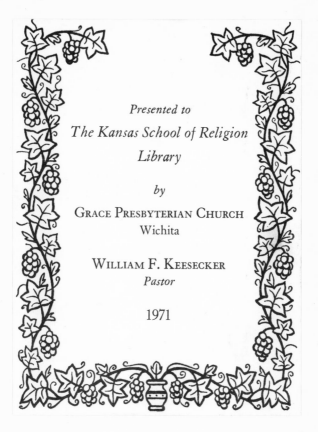

RELIGION, LANGUAGE AND TRUTH

BY THE SAME AUTHOR

Books
Christianity and Revolution *
The Future of Belief *
The Foundations of Belief *

Contributions to Books
Contraception and Holiness *
The Prospect of Change
Brief to the Bishops
Peace on Earth
The New Morality *
The Future of Belief Debate *
The Spectrum of Catholic Opinion
The Presence and Absence of God
God, Jesus and Spirit *

* Published by Herder and Herder

RELIGION, LANGUAGE AND TRUTH

Leslie Dewart

HERDER AND HERDER

1970
HERDER AND HERDER NEW YORK
232 Madison Avenue, New York 10016

Language - religious aspects
Christianity - philosophy

Library of Congress Catalog Card Number: 70–127870

Contents

Preface   9

PART I

PROBLEMS AND PRINCIPLES

1. Philosophy and Crisis   15
2. Language and Thought   29
3. Truth and Reality   63

PART II

ISSUES AND ILLUSTRATIONS

4. Faith and Experience   93
5. Church and Authority   107
6. Man and God   127

Appendix: Philosophy and the Limitations
  of Renewal   145

Index   171

For
L.M.A., E.J.A.,
C.S.M., C.M.G.,
and for
J.E.M.

Preface

A recent reviewer of my book, *The Foundations of Belief,* has
suggested that I should write "a short, popular statement of [my]
views, so that they may be made available to those [who may not
have a professional level of] technical and historical knowledge." [1]
I wish I could say that the present book responds to this request,
but in point of fact it goes only a short distance towards fulfilling
it. It is not that the objective does not attract me, but that I would
not want to undertake it lightly. It is much more difficult to write
for the "general public" than for the specialist, concisely than at
length, in outline than in detail. To do the latter requires no more
than some knowledge of one's subject; to do the former one must
have a mastery of it. While I keep open the possibility of writing
an elementary but thoughtful, brief but comprehensive, introduction to contemporary Christian philosophy from that viewpoint
which appears to me to commend itself today to the attention of
the Christian community, I have for the moment undertaken the
much less ambitious project of setting down, in a form and compass which the non-professional but industrious reader might not
find totally unacceptable (and with heavy reliance upon concrete
and practical issues which might illustrate them), only some of
the key ideas of which I have made use in my earlier work.

The general theme in which this book finds its context is the

[1] "The relative absolute," *Times Literary Supplement,* February 5, 1970,
p. 138.

9

view that philosophy today stands in a position from which it might signally contribute to the solution of the contemporary crisis of man, which I take to be an essentially "religious" one, the insight that religion in general, and belief in God in particular, have been deeply affected by the evolution of man, for this evolution has already brought about a change in the very nature of "religious" belief. To put it conversely, if we cannot readily identify and diagnose the problem of man in the twentieth century, much of the difficulty is that we do not recognize it as a religious problem—precisely because our common idea of religion is derived from what religion used to be in the past, rather than what it must be today, given the changes that have already affected the nature of man. The specific suggestion that I shall develop here, however, is that the nature of religious belief has changed in no way less profoundly than because man, becoming more aware of his own nature, has developed his understanding of what language is, and has therefore begun to revise his understanding of the relationship of language to reality and, therefore, his understanding of the nature of truth.

I have implied that I have tried to write this book keeping in mind that mythical and elusive, but in so many ways tangibly real person, the "general" reader who may have a great deal of interest in philosophical and religious questions, as well as a certain level of familiarity with the subject, but who is not a professional scholar and who has no more time to spend working his way through a book than he can snatch at the end of a busy and crowded work-day. He is a wraith, but I have met him; he is protean, but he exists; he is difficult to identify, but he reads books and, occasionally, reviews them in the general press. He has often asked me to speak to his circle or his group, his parish or his club, his friends or his colleagues. I like him, and I am grateful to him, and I want to tell him a thought or two that have occurred to me concerning our common problems and preoccupations. But he keeps vanishing before my eyes. Rather, I am not certain that in this book I have not at times turned my attention away from him, and gathered wool—and then spun it, and then allowed my substance and my prose to become emmeshed in it. Perhaps he will make my task easier if he will allow me to suggest how he might, if he wishes, proceed to read this book.

The thesis of the book is outlined in Chapter 1, and I imagine every reader will of course read it first. But Chapters 2 and 3 are given to an explanation of some of the basic principles of which I make use in the second part of the book. If the reader should find these chapters rather more theoretical than he deems personally useful, perhaps he should without any qualms turn immediately to Chapter 4 and read through to the end of the book. For at the beginning of this chapter I have recapitulated all the essential theoretical points of the first part, in order to preserve the continuity of the argument for a reader who had skipped Chapters 2 and 3—and in order to provide a convenient review for the reader who had not. Those who may have chosen the former alternative may well wish, after having encountered the ideas presented in these two chapters, but in much less abstract form, in the second part of the book, to return to them for a fuller understanding of the bases of the conclusions I have drawn.

Finally, I may note that this book is an expanded version—to about twice the original length—of a set of lectures commissioned by the Portland Christian Lectureship established jointly by the Roman Catholic Archdiocese of Portland (Oregon), Holy

Trinity Greek Orthodox Church of Portland, and the Greater Portland Council of Churches. I delivered the lectures in the First United Methodist Church of Portland in April, 1970, under the title "Human Reason, Christian Faith and Catholic Crisis." I am most grateful to the officers of the Lectureship, not only for the honour of having selected me as one of their annual Lecturers, but also for the kind and warm reception of which I was made the object during my pleasant and, from my viewpoint, all too brief stay in their midst. I also wish to acknowledge my debt and express my gratitude to Professor Peter Fitting, who has given me the benefit of his remarks on a number of points concerning linguistics.

To the revised text of the lectures I have appended a modified version of a paper I contributed to the First International Lonergan Congress held at the College of St. Leo, Florida, also in the Spring of 1970. The relevance of this paper to the theme of this book seemed to me sufficiently great to warrant its inclusion in this volume. For I thought that, by contrasting my own views on the subject of language and truth with other views I consider radically insufficient to the needs of contemporary Christianity, the meaning of what I have tried to express in these lectures would be all the clearer and easier to grasp.

PART I

PROBLEMS AND PRINCIPLES

1.

Philosophy and Crisis

For Christianity this is an ecumenical age. The variety of Christian viewpoints and traditions have within the last decade come to share the conviction that the things that join them, however limited their number, are much more fundamental and far more valuable than the things which divide them, however considerable their importance. Under these conditions my first thought is to open my remarks with an apology for addressing myself to topics which to all appearances will be not only non-ecumenical in substance, but which will seem even provincially Catholic in scope.

But on second thought I believe no such apology is really necessary. In most parts of the Christian world ecumenism appears to have been sufficiently successful already—that is, it has already produced enough spiritual unity in Christendom—to have rendered superfluous the Byzantine artificialities and symmetries which at one time, not so long ago, were considered strictly *de rigueur* wherever two or more denominations came together in dialogue. It is to the mutual advantage of all Christian traditions that we can now take for granted our common faith, that we neither crave nor, therefore, feel bound to offer, mutual reassurances of legitimacy, truth and the right to exist, and that we can now, therefore, unabashedly relish our differences. Pluralism no longer means merely friendly toleration, but also the inner freedom of Christian believers to put their varied denominational confessions to work for the common good. There is, indeed, a growing realization among Christians that juridical unity is not only a vain ecumenical goal, but that it might be actually undesirable, and that even liturgical, sacramental and doctrinal— not to speak of speculative—diversity might be a positive good. The day may yet come when the ecumenical movement may find it paradoxically necessary to promote the preservation of the multiplicity of Christian forms for the very sake of the spiritual unity of the Christian faith.

In a sense, therefore, my preoccupation with things Catholic, and in particular with the current crisis of the Catholic Church, a preoccupation which shall mark every one of these pages, is not only ecumenically excusable, but even ecumenically justified. Whatever is of real concern to any Christian denomination is of real concern to all. This would be true in any event, but it is especially applicable to the case at hand because, as I believe, the Catholic crisis is peculiarly Catholic only in its more superficial (if also in its more spectacular) manifestations. The Catholic crisis can be adequately understood only if it is studied within the context of a wider crisis affecting Christianity as a whole. And, indeed, this crisis may in turn be but part of a yet more fundamental crisis which involves human nature as a whole, a crisis which should be envisaged, if its true dimensions are to be appreciated, in terms of the processes of human evolution as a whole.

But the latter might be the topic of another book. I will leave it aside in order to deal with the narrower problems of Christianity, especially insofar as they are acutely manifested in the Catholic

Church. Allow me, then, to state and explain in some detail the thesis that I shall attempt to develop throughout this book, the theme to which all my remarks shall more or less directly refer.

I need not defend, I take it, the assumption under which I have been labouring so far, namely, that the Catholic Church *is* experiencing a crisis which threatens seriously to disrupt its unity and to jeopardize its effectiveness, if not also its viability. The contemporary Catholic crisis may well be the gravest crisis of the entire history of Christianity to date. And yet, when compared with, say, the Arian question, or the East-West schism, or the Reformation, the twentieth-century crisis of the Catholic Church is the most gratuitous of all, the least necessary or fateful, the likeliest one to have been avoided if only a few wise decisions had been taken in time. For this is, at one and the same time, a crisis which concerns the most basic questions of doctrine and practice, and yet a crisis which in itself does not hinge upon any one issue, any one doctrine of Christian belief nor, for that matter, on any number of doctrines or practices as such.

Indeed, if we raise the question: What is the Catholic crisis really about? the answer is far from obvious. It is easy, of course, to identify a number of interrelated topical matters which have temporarily captured public attention. Some of these have been practical: papal authority, clerical celibacy, liturgical innovations, due legal process, administrative and disciplinary order and, of course, the morality of contraception. Others have been highly theoretical, ranging from original sin to the nature of religion, and from the end of the world to the nature of God. But the very width of the spectrum of problems should reveal that the crisis cannot be defined in terms of the doctrines and practices of traditional Christian belief. The crisis, I suggest, has to do with

17

the very foundations of all the doctrines and practices of Christian belief.

When I refer to the foundations of belief what I have in mind is that all human conscious activity whatever is undergirded by certain assumptions, whether explicit or implicit, about *reality* and about *truth,* that is, about the world which exists about man, obtruding upon him and constituting his situation and locale, and about man's own relations to that world. Religious consciousness is no exception to this rule; all religious belief presupposes certain ideas about reality and truth. The contemporary Catholic crisis involves all possible doctrinal and practical questions, without hinging upon any one of them, because it actually has to do with the fundamental questions of the nature of reality and truth. This is what explains the paradoxical qualities of the crisis to which I have already alluded. Because it involves the very foundations of Christianity, this is the most serious crisis in the history of the Catholic Church and, indeed, in the history of Christianity as a whole. And yet, this is also the least fated, the most avoidable; it is, in principle, the most easily soluble crisis of all. Why is it so?

Well, consider the range of the profound divisions within the Catholic Church today. I have in mind not only the struggles and dissentions among the various factions, struggles which run the gamut from constructive, reasonable and civilized debates to disgraceful exhibitions in which arrogance tries to outdo impudence, and in which ignorance competes with bad manners for the prizes of vulgarity and ridicule. I also refer to the less spectacular, yet sadder, more unfortunate conflicts within the recesses of consciences and loyalties of many individual souls. If my suggestion is correct, these divisions really have to do, whether its

18

protagonists realize it or not, with the ideas of reality and truth. This means that the differences of opinion which operate in this, the gravest religious crisis of the Catholic Church, have at bottom to do not with theological or religious questions as such, but with the epistemological, metaphysical and other philosophical questions which underlie theological and religious disputes.

If Christianity were to take itself for a science, or for a philosophy, or for any other type of wisdom, knowledge or intellectual perfection created by the mind of man, then any conflict created by opposed philosophical or scientific viewpoints would indeed constitute an insurmountable religious division. But Christianity prides itself upon being a "revealed" religion. And however one may otherwise understand the nature of "revelation" there is no disagreement on at least this point: that in some sense or another Christianity derives its "salvific" efficacy, its essential truth, its value and validity as religion, not from the effectiveness of human understanding but from the self-communication of God. It would seem, then, that conflicts of religious opinion which stem from divergent philosophical views should be resoluble without great difficulty and without any compromise on matters of religious principle. Surely, one would think, as long as the divisions really have to do with philosophical questions, which do not pertain to revelation, religious unity need not be jeopardized. To be sure, philosophical diversity would continue to obtain. But if those who diverged philosophically agreed at least on the subordination of philosophical thought to religious belief—in the sense that they recognized the fallibility of all human reason and the contingency of all human opinion—then philosophical divergence should not impair the unity of Christian belief.

And yet, a satisfactory solution of the Catholic crisis is far from

19

assured. Indeed, unless new factors were to affect the situation, such a solution seems at present not a little unlikely. For the resolution of the crisis need not of itself demand any doctrinal or moral compromise on anyone's part. But this counts for nothing if the adherents of one (or, for that matter, the other) philosophical opinion nevertheless imagine that, despite the revealed character of Christianity and the contingency of all human wisdom in general, their particular philosophical opinions have a peculiar privileged connection with the Christian faith and that, therefore, to diverge from their all-too-human and essentially fallible philosophical views is, as it so happens, to diverge from the truths revealed by God.

The reasoning that produces this conclusion is very curious; as I reconstruct it, it goes like this. It is true that there is no revealed epistemology or metaphysics and, more generally, that human opinions do not, of course, have any source other than man's own natural powers, and that they are in no sense revealed by God. It is also true that revelation does not provide a scientific account of the world, and that it does not substitute for scientific or even for everyday, common sense knowledge. Moreover, it is true that revelation does not imply any unique cultural context, or language, or mode of apprehension, or vocabulary, or any other strictly human concept, opinion, idea, theory or view. On the other hand, the argument continues, two stipulations should nevertheless be made. First: not every philosophical or scientific theory is compatible with the truth of revelation; not every vocabulary or cultural context is equally hospitable to the truth of revelation; not every human opinion is tenable in the light of what God has revealed. And since the source of revelation is a higher intellect than man's, it follows that he who is enlightened

20

by faith in revelation is in a position to judge, at least negatively, concerning the truths of human science, philosophy or everyday opinion, insofar as these should manifestly contradict those of revelation. Second: there may be certain human opinions, certain scientific views and, above all, certain philosophical theories and concepts, whose truth may require protection by Christianity, because they are of special relevance to the truth of revelation. Although these philosophical matters remain the proper object of human reason, and may not be said to have been revealed, the truth discovered by human reason in their regard may be affirmed by the believer, not only because it is supported by evidence or experience, but also, once it is supported by evidence or experience, because it is supported by its privileged connection with matters of faith. For since the human truth in question is true and logically necessary in order to uphold truths of faith, to deny this human truth is implicitly to deny the Christian faith in the revelation of God.

I am reminded at this point of a true story, an exchange that took place during the deliberations of the Papal Commission on Birth Control. It appears that someone, scandalized at the suggestion that the Church could at this late date declare contraception to be morally permissible, exclaimed: "What then of the millions we have up to now sent to hell, if these things can be changed?" To which Mrs. Patrick Crowley, the charming co-President of the Christian Family Movement, replied: "But, sir, are you sure that God has always executed all your orders?"

The parallel between the views expressed in connection with this moral problem by the theologian in question and the views I have been analyzing regarding the general relation between human reason and divine revelation is more than superficial. For

21

this theologian, I imagine, did actually believe the proposition which, to Mrs. Crowley as to many other people, sounds not merely ridiculous but perhaps even blasphemous and in any event arrogant: that God will submit to human judgment. For, if we consider again the arguments I have reproduced above, we may have to grant that despite their concern with safeguarding the truth of revelation, what they actually affirm in the end is that certain human opinions are guaranteed by the truth of revelation—in effect, that God will uphold certain judgments made by certain men.

Let us grant that not every human opinion is compatible with the truth of revelation. The judgment whether any given opinion is or is not compatible with the truth of revelation is itself a human opinion. If God published a periodical bulletin rating current releases of human thought as, say, "Approved for all," "Objectionable in part," "Condemned," and "Judgment pending due to recency of appearance," then it would be more reasonable to think that a judgment made by human logic about the incompatibility of some given view with revelation enjoys the same certitude and authority as revelation. To put it more precisely, the judgment that certain human opinions are incompatible with revelation is not itself a revealed truth: it is a human judgment. It may be a correct judgment; it may well be a legitimately made judgment; it might even be an authoritative judgment. But it remains a human judgment. The judgment that a certain human opinion is incompatible with the truth of revelation is a judgment *about* revelation. But it is not revelation; it remains a *human* judgment about revelation. The fact that it is about revelation does not make it less human than if it were about anything else.

Likewise, granted that some philosophical or scientific theories may well in fact be less appropriate than others for the conceptualization and development of Christian doctrine, the opinion that any given theory or concept is particularly apt—or, for that matter, particularly unsuitable—for this purpose depends upon one's evaluation of the adequacy and truth of such theory or concept. To be sure, one could scarcely affirm one's philosophical or common sense opinions without implying that they appear to be true and, therefore, that they appear to be the most appropriate for the conceptualization and development of Christian doctrine. But this opinion has no more authority behind it than the like opinion of someone else who holds different views. It is one thing to say that certain ideas which one holds to be correct have a special theological or religious relevance. It is quite another to say that because one's ideas are true, they therefore have a special theological or religious relevance. The first is a legitimate value judgment; the second is reason's usurpation of the mantle of religious faith. Unfortunately, many people who are otherwise intelligent and undoubtedly well disposed cannot tell the difference between the two and, therefore, with none but the best intentions, but with the arrogant humility of him who credits God for having made him to have a privileged judgment, erect their human opinions into the practical equivalent of a criterion of religious truth.

The difficulty is that, precisely because they are in good faith, they will meet every opinion contrary to theirs with the impenetrably dogmatic argument that such contrary views, being mistaken, could not possibly advance the cause of religious truth. In short, we have to do here with basically the same phenomenon that produced the Galileo case in the seventeenth century, the reaction against Darwin in the nineteenth, and the condemnation of almost every other scientific discovery in between. The only difference is that the tragic confusion reaches yet deeper levels today. For what I have said so far about philosophical, scientific and common sense opinions in general applies with special force to the fundamental concepts of reality and truth. Many Catholics today, especially among those in positions of high authority, are, more or less consciously, of the opinion that only the traditional ideas of truth and reality can possibly serve as the foundations of Christian belief and that, therefore, faith dictates *a priori* the rejection of the possibility of alternatives to traditional Catholic philosophical thought.

There is, I believe, an invalid transition in this reasoning, illustrating what I have already described. If natural reason suggests that the traditional concepts of truth and reality are alone true, it does follow that only the traditional concepts of truth and reality are compatible with the true faith. But this is itself a conclusion of human reason, and it is valid if, and only if, the traditional philosophical views are themselves true. The conclusion is, therefore, subject to doubt and possible refutation within the limits of strict adherence to Christian belief. Many people, however, sever this proposition from its philosophical origin and, attending only to its matter, hold it as a matter of faith. Yet, this involves not only a breach of rational values, but also of those of faith, since it amounts to the elevation of certain opinions of human reason to the practical status of revealed truths. Thus, the crisis cannot be easily resolved, even if it hinges on issues that pertain to human opinion, because many people in the Church, particularly among those in authority, have for all practical purposes invested merely philosophical views with the certitude of faith and the authority of revelation.

24

Almost any instance we took would bring us to the same conclusion. Perhaps I should mention, however, the issue of contraception. Though I hesitate to introduce this threadbare topic once again, it is one of the most obvious instances of what I mean. In the last analysis the real questions here have been decided not only on the basis of underlying attitudes towards sexuality, but above all in the light of certain ideas about the nature of truth. I believe this is true, in the first place, of those Catholics who have reached a conclusion contrary to the official teaching of the Church but who nevertheless believe themselves to remain in communion with the Roman Catholic Church. But it is also true, I think, of the highest magisterium of the Church.

The position taken by *Humanae Vitae* is unavoidable once it is granted that sexuality is an especially sacred part of human nature —that is, a part of it which stands aside from all others, and which has a special relationship to the transcendent; or, if you wish, that God has a special interest in sex. Yet, what is truly curious about this document is that, despite its underlying attitude towards sexuality, its relative openness towards the possibility of change in this very respect is remarkably great. This is especially evident in its avoidance of the terms "primary" and "secondary" with reference to the ends of marriage, and its treatment of the "unitive" and "procreative" sexual functions on the basis of equality—albeit also on the basis of inseparability. The real intransigeance of the encyclical is rather revealed in those sections which, in my opinion, provide the real preponderance of the document's conclusion against the morality of contraception. I refer to the sections which assume, in effect, that belief in the truth of Christianity forbids the possibility of a practical judgment on the matter which were substantially at variance with past official doctrine. For, apparently, the essential truth of the matter could not change. If contraception was intrinsically wrong in the past, it will remain intrinsically wrong forever. And to suggest that the Church taught wrongly in the past in connection with such a serious matter would be to suggest that there is no truth to Christianity now, and that there never was any truth to it in the past. If it is admitted that the Church has erred in the past, its total teaching authority is effectively denied.

Conversely, the vast majority of Catholics who, retaining their Catholic faith, have decided for themselves in opposition to *Humanae Vitae,* have done so, as best one can estimate, only on the basis of certain novel attitudes towards sexuality. But by and large they seem to have had little hesitation as to how they really felt about the sexual problem itself. The more fundamental difficulty they had to overcome had rather to do with their assessment of their own relationship to the teaching authority of a Church whose doctrine they nevertheless believed to be somehow true.

But it is, of course, the issue of clerical celibacy, where it is granted on all sides that no absolute doctrinal bar exists to a change in the discipline, that most clearly of all brings out the real problem, namely, that the conflicts of the Catholic crisis are shaped by the most dangerous good faith of all: the good faith of those who believe that their judgment enjoys special religious prerogatives. And this they must believe if, side by side with their faith in the truth and validity of Christianity and in the legitimacy of Church authority, they retain the traditional outlook upon the nature of man and of the world to which man stands bound in the closest relationship.

What is a viable alternative outlook upon man and his relation to reality, and upon the world of reality in which man lives? This will be the topic of discussion in the next two chapters, before we turn, in the second part of the book, to a consideration of how this alternative would affect some of the key concepts of Christian religious belief. It may come as a surprise to anyone who has not had an opportunity to follow closely the course of recent scholarship that one of the most fruitful approaches to this topic is the study of what is, if we but reflect upon it, at the heart of all that is distinctively human: the phenomenon of speech.

2.

Language and Thought

One of the most significant contributions to man's understanding of himself and of his relationship to the world—the environment of reality in which he is situated—has been the gradual discovery, more or less simultaneously made by many different disciplines during the twentieth century, that the assumptions long held by our culture's intellectual tradition concerning the nature of language are not quite correct and must be, therefore, revised. We are only beginning to realize, however, how far-reaching may be the consequences of this revision. For we are only beginning to explore the implications of the reorientation of our thinking concerning the human phenomenon of speech.

Perhaps we can best approach the subject by considering in the first place how Western thought has traditionally understood the nature of language, after which we may examine some of the difficulties that have accrued to this view in the course of Western man's intellectual development. Now, this traditional idea of language might with some justice be called the Aristotelian view, not because Aristotle was by any means its originator, but because he was one of the first philosophers to have stated it clearly and systematically. There is in particular a stark and pithy Aristotelian text which has had a historical influence in our culture, down to our own day, the extent of which would be difficult to exaggerate. I refer to Aristotle's statement that

spoken words are the signs of mental experience and written words are the signs of spoken words. Just as all men have not the same writing, so all men have not the same speech sounds, but the mental experiences, which these directly signify, are the same for all, as also are those things of which our experiences are the images. . . . By a noun we mean a sound significant by convention.[1]

But this view might somewhat more descriptively be called the *semantic* interpretation of language,[2] since its essential feature is the idea that words are the outward *sign* of inner experience or thought. This refers in the first instance to spoken words, for speech, the system of signs that express and translate mental activity from within to without, may in turn be expressed and translated from a transitory and fleeting to a stable and relatively more permanent form by another system of signs operative at a higher level, namely, written words. Writing, then, signifies speech directly, and thought or inner experience only indirectly, that is, by first signifying speech, which in turn signifies thought. Spoken words, however, signify the mind's experience of reality directly.

According to this view, since the reality which is the object of mental experience is one and the same for all beholders, it follows

[1] *On Interpretation*, 1 (16 a 3–19). The most common translations of this text use "symbol" where I have used "sign." I have elsewhere (*The Foundations of Belief*, [New York, 1969], pp. 93–94) explained why, given contemporary English usage, "sign" may be a more faithful rendering than "symbol."

[2] From the Greek, *semeion*, "sign," "signal," "token," "mark," "flag," "omen," "trace," etc. I might, with perhaps slightly greater etymological justification, have also called it the *semiotic* theory of languages, but the term *semantic* is of much greater currency and of sufficient aptness to serve my purposes well.

that the mental experience of that reality must be correspondingly the same for all men. There is, thus, a sort of natural and necessary connection between a mental experience and the reality of which it is the experience. When the mind is presented with, say, a table, it must experience a table if it is going to experience at all: when one stands in front of a table one cannot arbitrarily decide that one is going to experience, say, a chair—unless perhaps one's mind were utterly deranged. This means that there is a radical distinction between language and thought, since men use a variety of vocal sounds(*mensa, Tisch, wei*) to express and signify their common experience of one and the same thing, the table. Of course, the same is true of the written signs used to signify the spoken signs. These signs have no natural or necessary connection with the experience of which they are the signs. They are signs by convention—and frequently indeed by arbitrary convention— among men, in order to communicate with each other and, as it were, share their inner experience of the world.

This understanding of language is so deeply rooted in our culture and its linguistic and other institutions that what I have just stated in behalf of Plato and Aristotle appears to us naturally as elementary common sense. It would seem that although much might be added to this interpretation of the nature of language by way of further explanation, nothing could be taken away from it without falling into absurdity and without contradicting the most obvious observations about the linguistic behaviour of men. And yet, it would be no exaggeration to say that there is scarcely any important novel concept of recent scholarship that does not, more or less directly, more or less radically, tend to contradict it. The most diverse lines of enquiry frequently converge upon the conclusion that the semantic concept of language simply cannot be

31

reconciled with what happens in reality. Whatever else language might be, it is not a system of signs which stand for, or represent, or express, man's experience of reality. While there may not be among contemporary scholars any consensus approaching unanimity concerning what language positively is, there is widespread, if not fairly general, dissatisfaction with the supposed obviousness of the Aristotelian view.

The semantic conception of language is at odds, for instance, with a thorough-going understanding of the social nature of man. I say *thorough-going* because, as it so happens, it was also Aristotle who first said that "man is a social animal." But it is doubtful if he meant more than this: that, once human nature is essentially determined in individual reality, the exercise of human life could not be successfully undertaken except in the society of other men —and language is precisely one of the means whereby men can lead a common life. I say it is doubtful because in this philosophy the nature of man is not actually social, but individual. For it is only under this condition that language can be reduced, as it is reduced by Aristotle, to communication. The assumption made by the semantic idea of language is that man does not need language to be human, but only to share with other men the human experience of his individual human nature, and thus facilitate his other social relations. On the other hand, it is much more difficult today than in Aristotle's day to grant to human nature the individual self-sufficiency that this would imply. We shall consider this in more detail below. For the moment let us merely wonder whether man could be human, in any significant and realistic sense of the term, if he were complete in his own silent nature, without speech, and as if speech were really outside the sphere of his substantial existence. Is it true that man, the human, speaks in order to be social? Or is it not that man, the animal, speaks in order to be human? If society is not the proliferation but the matrix of human nature, language is not the excrescence but the seed of the human soul.

Though the argument I have just presented is actually quite important, it is not likely at first sight to carry nearly as much conviction as does this other: it is difficult to reconcile the traditional idea of language with the evolutionary approach to the study of man. The semantic interpretation of language assumes that although individuals have to learn to speak, mankind as a whole has always known how to do so. For it is an assumption of the Aristotelian view that in order to learn how to speak it is enough to learn which signs to use, according to the currency in one's social environment, for the purpose of designating certain experiences—and that, therefore, anyone who is human is by that very fact already in a position to use signs in order to designate given experiences. In other words, the semantic interpretation assumes that to learn to speak all one has to do is to learn *a* language—thus, in effect, that human beings know how to speak before they learn any language. Or, again, that one learns one's first language in the same way in which one learns one's second.[3]

The difficulty here is that this presupposes, if not that human society has always known some language which the individual can learn when he is born to that society, at least that men have always had the ability to speak, even before they devised, "by convention," the original signs whereby to exteriorize and share their human experience. Needless to say, the assumption of an evolutionary standpoint would preclude any such presupposition.

[3] That is, if one learns it by the inefficient method of translating from one's own language into another.

33

Even if the individual human being were able to speak before actually knowing any language—and we shall look at the matter more closely in a moment—mankind as a whole has had to acquire the ability to use (let us for the present continue to call them) significant vocal sounds: mankind has had to learn not only a language, but to speak. Indeed, mankind's devising of the various human languages could in reality have been but mankind's acquisition of linguistic ability, of the power to speak. Man had to create not merely the supposedly conventional signs of language, but the very possibility of creating conventional signs. Thus, it may well be that men do use conventional signs—and this not only in the realm of non-vocal signs, like arrows and traffic lights, but even in the realm of certain levels of language.[4] It is quite another thing, however, to say that language as such is a system of conventional signs.

The weight of this proposition is not on *conventional,* but on *signs.* For if words truly are signs, then it must be granted that they also are, by and large, conventional in some sense. No one in his right mind is likely to maintain that the "real" name of tables is *table,* rather than *mensa* or *Tisch.* Now, as long as we ignore the evolutionary dimension of man and abstain from raising every question concerning the development of human speech, the conventionality of linguistic signs causes no further problem. If, on the contrary, evolution is presupposed, then the semantic conception of language lands us in self-contradiction. Language cannot be a system of signs, precisely because, as Aristotle rightly understood, if it is a system of signs, it must be a system of conventional signs. But the difficulty with the latter proposition is that although

[4] For instance, when we say "let x stand for y," or "I dub thee Sir Pentine," or "Thou art Cephas."

some signs, and even some linguistic signs, as I have granted, can actually have the character of conventional signs, language as such may not have such character, if it is true that language is an evolutionary phenomenon. (And if human nature as a whole is the emergent product of an evolutionary process, it follows that linguistic ability must be considered to have been developed by man in the course of human evolution.)

The reason is that the very concept of conventional sign *presupposes* that of language. That is, the definition of language as a system of signs is circular, for no one could suppose that language is a system of signs unless he first knew what language does. Of course, if what language does is to signify reality (or, more precisely, to signify our experience of reality, which in turn signifies reality), it does follow that words are signs. Conversely, we can construe words as signs only if we first divorce words from speech and treat them as if they had an independent *linguistic* reality. We can, to be sure, regard words strictly from the viewpoint of their independent reality—that is, as a sound of a certain complex modulation, or as a pattern of a certain colour and shape in the case of written words. But insofar as we do this we disregard the *linguistic* import of words. A parrot does not talk. Nor does a tape recorder. The semantic concept of language implies that whereas mankind has learned to use certain specific sounds for linguistic purposes, mankind has not developed linguistic purposes but, presumably, has always had them.

Thus, it will not do to imagine that mankind devised language by the same expedient, writ but large, which *we* (who *already* know how to speak) could nowadays use—though, at most, under severe restrictions and for strictly limited purposes—in order to devise a system of conventional signs. For example, *we* could do

35

so by pointing to a table and uttering, for someone else's benefit, the sound *Tisch*—or by telling the fledgling driver that the green light means "go" and the red light means "stop." For there are, in addition to language, codes and translations. But codes and translations can be such only because language undergirds them. The transformations of stereotyped translations (table = *Tisch,* or *Comment allez vous* = How do you do ≠ How do you go) are possible only by virtue of a prior understanding of the translation. (That is, either one *knows* what the translated expression means, or else one takes for it the word of someone who does understand what it means.[5]) Likewise, the convention by which a common meaning is assigned to a certain sign is possible only by virtue of a prior "convention," namely, a convention about the meaning of pointing, or of labelling, or indeed of *sign,* and, more generally, about the meaning of language and communication.

The point I am trying to make could be put more graphically, albeit somewhat facetiously, as follows. If language were a system of conventional signs, the creation of language by convention would have required a prior convention about what language is. But such a prior convention would itself have required communication—and, therefore, a yet prior convention to devise the language of such communication, and so on *ad infinitum.* Nowadays, when human beings already know how to speak and when

[5] For instance, *Comment allez vous,* which ordinarily should be translated as "How do you do," may sometimes require "How do you go." There is no way to tell from an examination of this sentence which these two mutually exclusive translations is the correct one: to know the right translation it is necessary first to know what is meant. In actual use, of course, there would hardly be a real problem as to which actually fits, because the context makes the meaning clear. The point is precisely that the context is necessary to grasp the meaning. All but the simplest translations are living refutations of the semantic theory of language.

they have languages, they could hold conventions to create new languages—but they could do this only because they already have an old language which they could use in their working sessions in order to create new languages. But it is not easy to imagine how people could hold a convention to create their first language. In what language would they have conducted the proceedings? And how would they have agreed in the first place that human convention could create language? The Aristotelian view of language is plausible only so long as human evolution is left out of account.

A parallel, equally insurmountable difficulty has been encountered by a number of linguists and other students of the psychology of language-learning. It would appear that the Aristotelian concept of language is incompatible not only with the idea that the linguistic abilities of mankind as a whole have emerged through evolution, but even with the supposition that the individual himself learns how to speak. For, in effect, if the semantic concept of language is correct, the child does not actually learn to speak but, rather, having been born knowing how to speak (though ignorant of any and all semantic systems), all he needs to learn in order to communicate is how to use the signs of a certain given linguistic semantic system. Thus, if learning to speak were but learning to associate certain signs and their corresponding experiences, learning to speak would not be the acquisition of a linguistic function, but simply the acquisition of the facility to exercise a linguistic function which the newborn already possesses as a sort of innate faculty. But why, it might well be asked, could this not be precisely the case? Why could the child not have an innate potentiality for speaking which is actualized only when, and as, he learns to associate certain sounds with certain experiences? Or, taking the opposite tack—which, however, leads to the same destination—why could one not say that there is no distinction whatever between learning how to speak and learning to use a certain language, so that learning to associate given sounds with given experiences *is* learning to speak, and that only after one learns to use sounds for purposes of signification does one generalize to the abstract idea of "sign" in general, or of "language"?

Many psychologists, particularly among the behaviourists, have long held, in line with the long philosophical tradition, that the mechanism of learning to speak is indeed associative, probably that mechanism known as the "conditioning" of responses. What further reflection has revealed—and in this connection the name of Noam Chomsky could not be altogether omitted [6]—is, however,

---

[6] From the viewpoint of the philosophy of language Chomsky's distinction among the linguists of the English-speaking world consists in his having forcefully recalled to the attention of linguistic research the creative (as contrasted with the repetitive) character of language: "The limitless possibilities of thought and imagination are reflected in the creative aspect of language use. The language provides finite means but infinite possibilities of expression" (*Cartesian Linguistics,* [New York, 1966], p. 29). At bottom, this contradicts the semantic interpretation of language. Nevertheless, Chomsky reverts to semanticism when he supposes that language has "an abstract deep structure determining its semantic content and a surface structure determining its phonetic form. A complete grammar, then, would consist of a finite system of rules generating this infinite set of paired structures and thus showing how the speaker-hearer can make infinite use of finite means in expressing his 'mental acts' and 'mental states'" (*ibid.* p. 52). By the same token, Chomsky believes that, for instance, the translatability of every natural language into every other natural language points to the existence of "linguistic universals," that is, universal, constant, essentially invariable *antecedents* of linguistic development and performance which make up "the initial assumptions concerning the nature of language that the child brings to language learning," (*Aspects of the Theory of Syntax,* [Cambridge, Mass., 1965], p. 27). Conversely there are "aspects of

that in order to learn to speak the child has to learn not simply
the significative value of any given set of words, but the various

the base structure [of language which] . . . pertain to the form of language in general rather than to the form of particular languages, and
thus presumably reflect what the mind brings to the task of language
acquisition rather than what it discovers (or invents) in the course of
carrying out this task," (*ibid.*, p. 117).

Chomsky is forced to paper over this inconsistent reversion to what I
have here called semanticism with the supposition that there is a specifically
linguistic potentiality in the individual, (cf. *Language and Mind,* [New
York, 1968], pp. 24, 72, 74 *et passim*), so that learning to "use" language
creatively means precisely that: not the mind's acquisition of a linguistic
faculty, but the linguistic faculty's acquisition of the syntactic skills and
other means whereby the mind can express outwardly its prior experience.
That is, the power to speak is not itself developed out of the potentialities
implicit in the living human organism; it is an "innate property," an innate faculty. This refers, of course, to the individual's linguistic faculty.
Chomsky's supposition is subject, therefore, to the objection that it begs
the question how mankind as a whole acquired this faculty in the course
of human evolution. He takes refuge in the statement that "the processes
by which the human mind achieved its present stage of complexity and its
particular form of innate organization are a total mystery . . . It is perfectly safe to attribute this development to 'natural selection,' so long as
we realize that there is no substance to this assertion, that it amounts to
nothing more than a belief that there is some naturalistic explanation for
these phenomena," (*ibid.*, p. 83). I should have thought, however, that it
amounted to at least a little more, namely, to the belief that some naturalistic explanation accounted for the *emergence* of these phenomena
through a process of evolutionary development. If we assume that humanity
is the result of an evolutionary process, the linguistic "faculty" can be, no
more than any other specifically human characteristic, innate in mankind,
in human nature as such.

Chomsky's inconsistency is the fairly typical result of the inability of
linguists since Wilhelm von Humbdoldt in the early nineteenth century to
translate their objections to the Aristotelian view of language into a
linguistic theory which altogether avoided the seemingly unavoidable and
fixed datum that language is a system of signs. Hence, the contributions of
linguists in the twentieth century have been directed towards the goal of
modifying, qualifying and improving upon the Aristotelian interpretation,
without criticizing its root. This is true, for instance, of Ferdinand de
Saussure, one of the founding fathers of "structuralism," for whom the

linguistic functions of significant sounds in general, and that the significative value of words may be apprehended only on the presupposed awareness of their linguistic function. If we study

linguistic sign "unites, not a thing and a name, but a concept and an acoustic image," so that language is "a unity with two faces" (*Cours de linguistique générale*, [Paris, 1915], p. 145). De Saussure's distinction between the "significant" and the "signified" aspects of language (the *signifiant*, i.e. the acoustic image, and the *signifié*, i.e. the concept) has been reproduced with further refinement but without radical change by the best known among the more recent writers on linguistics—for instance, by Louis Hjelmslev: "That a language is a system of signs seems *a priori* an evident and fundamental proposition, which linguistic theory will have to take into account at an early stage. Linguistic theory must be able to tell us what meaning can be attributed to this proposition, and especially to the word *sign*" (*Prolegomena to a Theory of Language*, [Madison, 1961], p. 43). Hjelmslev ends up distinguishing the linguistic "purport" of the mind, which in itself is "amorphous," and the linguistic "form" that concretizes it. For instance, if we consider a variety of sentences in different languages, such as *I do not know, je ne sais pas*, etc., we may observe that "despite all their differences, [they] have a factor in common, namely, the purport, the thought itself" (*ibid.*, p. 50). The assumption here is that the "purport" is logically and genetically (though not necessarily chronologically) prior to its specific "form," since the "purport" is given "form" in order that it may be *expressed*. It follows that "the same purport is formed or structured differently in different languages. What determines its form is solely the functions of the language," and that the form "is independent of, and stands in arbitrary relation to, the *purport*" (*ibid.*, p. 52). I find it difficult to detect any essential difference between this "purport" and the "intention" of Scholastic logic, or between this "arbitrary relation" and Aristotle's "conventional" relation of the name to the concept.

At the other end of the same dilemma stand those like Franz Boas, Edward Sapir and Benjamin Whorf, whose approach to linguistics from the vantage point of cultural anthropology led them to the insight that if the purport, mental intention or thought is truly determined by its linguistic form, then the purport, intention or thought cannot possibly remain "the same" when it receives different forms, but is indeed different to the very degree that it is structured differently by different linguistic forms—precisely because it is structured differently by different forms. But these authors retained the "evident" idea that language can be nothing but a system of signs—since cognition can be nothing but the mind's signification to itself of an outer meaning existing in reality. Therefore, their "cultural actual linguistic behaviour, we can observe that even after people know how to speak and use a language the semantic role of the words they use presupposes their prior ability to recognize their

relativism" has been open to the criticism that it implies in turn an inconsistency of its own: all modes of thinking and perceiving are equivalent, yet mutually incompatible. Or, again, since all forms of experience are equally valid they must be essentially untranslatable from one culture (or linguistic system) to another. But if they are essentially untranslatable (as, indeed, they would be, *if* the assumption were retained that experience precedes language and is subsequently expressed by speech) and if, therefore, they are not precisely equivalent, the various forms of culturally conditioned human experience are not really equally valid. They are, rather, one and all equally invalid. Being untranslatable (except, of course, approximately and distortedly), the supposed validity of each culturally conditioned form of experience would refute the actual validity of all.

The first traditional premise that required revision before the Aristotelian interpretation of language could be transcended was the priority of inner thought over outer speech. Eugen Rosenstock-Huessy was among the first (1945) to suggest that "languages are not means by which we represent the truth after it is perceived, but . . . means to discover hitherto ignored truth" (*Speech and Reality*, [Norwich, 1970], p. 172). But this hypothesis is unviable unless another traditional premise is also revised. For it is true that one cannot very well transcend the semantic view of language while retaining the semantic view of consciousness—but one cannot possibly transcend the semantic view of consciousness while retaining the semantic interpretation of reality.

We shall consider this in more detail in the next chapter. Meanwhile I will but note that Jacques Derrida is one of the few students of linguistics who have realized that the ultimate foundation of every semantic interpretation of language is the tacit or explicit metaphysical assumption that reality as such is constituted by a signifiable content. "All the conceptual oppositions of metaphysics," he has suggested, such as the opposition between the *signifiant* and the *signifié*, or between the sensible and the intelligible, etc., stem from the subordination of the mind's process of differentiation (*la différance*) [sic] "to the presence of a [supposed] value or *meaning* which would be anterior to [the process of] differentiation, and more primitive than it, and which would in the last analysis exceed it and subjugate it" ("Sémiologie et grammatologie," *Information sur les sciences sociales*, VII [1968], 3, 135–148; p. 144. Cf. his *De la grammatologie*, [Paris 1967], esp. pp. 106–108).

syntactic [7] function. That is, the semantics of a language presuppose that language's syntax. One cannot learn to use words in their correct signification (i.e. signifying what they commonly signify) unless one knows something about the way in which such words can be put together.

For example, the word *table* can be said to be the correct sign for a table, but only in the context of a language which, for instance, uses nouns as a distinct "part of speech." To learn to use the word *table* as the sign for a table is not merely to learn to use it in reference to tables rather than in reference to chairs: it is to learn to use it, for instance, as a noun rather than as a verb. Or perhaps it should be put the other way about: the word *table* can be said to be a sign of certain pieces of furniture only because it can function as such a sign within a syntactic context. Thus, it is only *after* one knows how to speak that one may consider any given word to act as a sign. If so, learning to speak is not the same as learning to use a certain vocabulary with correct reference to its corresponding assemblage of things in the world. For a real-life, functioning language cannot be constructed out of a vocabulary alone. One needs, *in the first place,* the grammatical rules that make up the language [8] which in turn has a certain vocabulary (which, incidentally, unlike the basic rules is extremely volatile and subject to arbitration). In conclusion: a language is not

[7] From the Greek, *syntaxis,* the action of "grouping together," or "arranging together."

[8] I have put this somewhat imprecisely. Clearly, grammatical *rules* are ascertained and abstracted from a reflective study of the way in which the language actually functions. It would be as absurd to suppose that language was devised by syntactic convention as by semantic convention. The point is that at the heart of language, underlying its semantics, there is a "grammar," and specifically a "syntax," that is, a *linguistic function* which cannot be reduced to the signification of experience by vocal sounds.

derived from a vocabulary by inductive generalization; on the contrary, a vocabulary is derived from a language by particularizing abstraction. Language is not a collection of vocables or vocal signs, but such a way of using vocal sounds that they can appear, upon reflection, as the vicar of, or as the label for, or as the pointer to—that is, as the sign of—that which is experienced by the mind.

Once again we reach through the study of individual development (ontogenesis) the same sort of conclusion previously suggested by considerations pertaining to the development of the (human) genus as a whole (phylogenesis). Language cannot be related to experience as the sign is to the signified unless language were reduced to the mouthing or vocalization of *meaningless* sounds which, (not without some self-contradiction), nevertheless *meant* the experience of reality held by the mind. For vocalization does not of itself make the vocal sounds to be significant. There must be, therefore, an anterior (that is, a more fundamental, a logically prior) linguistic function, namely, the function of signification, which makes the vocal sounds to be significant. But this linguistic function would be, of course, a language without words, or a speech without language, or a signifying without signs—an absurdity the self-contradictory nature of which should be readily evident. It is true that there must be a linguistic function which underlies vocalization—but this linguistic function cannot possibly be semantic. Language cannot be a system of vocal signs.

The positive suggestion that emerges from these negative remarks will be elaborated in due course later in this lecture and especially in the next; but perhaps it is not too early to lead into it. Although anyone who can speak is capable of learning, devising and decoding codes, speech is not the ability to learn, devise

43

and decode codes, because speech is the ground of all possible learning, devising and decoding of codes. Speech, therefore, must be understood not as the signification of the experience of reality, but as that function of experience which makes the signs of reality to be significant. Speech is, if you will, not making signs, but making signs to be significant. More precisely, speech is not making signs (which signs would be significant, if not by themselves, at least by convention), but rendering signs significant (which signs become significant not because they are signs but, on the contrary, which signs become signs only because they signify). But once we suppose that this is what language is, namely, this function whereby man relates himself to reality, it is difficult to distinguish it from thought, so that, as we shall see below, language should be conceived as the vocal, creative form of thought. This means: language does *not* give substance or concrete structure to a formless *but prior* mental reality or thought. On the contrary, linguistic form is the condition of the possibility of thought.

Meanwhile let us consider certain other implications of the semantic interpretation of language. To say that language is essentially the use of sounds to signify our experience of reality is to say that language is a means of communicating, that is, of expressing outwardly, our inner, self-contained experience. The assumption here is that first we experience, and then we project that experience beyond ourselves. Our experience is complete, precisely as experience, before it is exteriorized. Language, therefore, adds nothing to experience as such: human experience remains the same whether man speaks or not, and regardless of what he may say about it. Thus, language and experience may be correlative, but they are distinct and separate realities: what is said is one thing, meaning it is another. This, too, would appear to be elementary common sense, and it is difficult to imagine that any suggestion to the contrary should be seriously entertained.

Once again, however, the self-evidence and unquestionableness of the Aristotelian approach to language have suffered considerably as a result of studies on the nature of the so-called means of communication. All the indications that have emerged in this connection point to the inadequacy of the traditional view of language. For the idea that there can be in reality some experience, something-to-be-said, apart from, if not indeed prior to, the saying of it, is contradicted by the observable facts, if only we consider them closely: what is communicated is intrinsically dependent, for its very content, upon the "means" of communication. In Marshall McLuhan's well-known formula, "the medium is the message."

McLuhan's way of putting it incorporates the exaggeration that is usually happily tolerated in epigrams. The substance of it, nevertheless, withstands serious criticism. McLuhan's *bon mot* implies that communication cannot be correctly construed as the signification of a signified by means of a sign—rather, it is the "extension of man" into his environment—since the function of signification is precisely what is communicated by means of signs. Conversely, a sign can be a "means" of communication only because of what is signified by the function of signification. For if "the medium is the message", it follows that the message is also the medium. There are, if you will, no *media* of communication: there are only messages. Rather, the only means of human communication is linguistic behaviour itself. But this assumes that communication is not the mere conveying of experience. Communication is intrinsic part of experience. As it were, the message is the mind. Let us consider this at greater length.

McLuhan's work strikes at the root of the Aristotelian under-

45

standing of language at a yet deeper level than we had studied so far. For it would seem as if at least one aspect of Aristotle's semantic view of language had remained untouched by the line of criticism I had followed so far. That is, even if my previous observations are correct, it would seem that Aristotle was right in any event to assume that the essence of language is to be found strictly realized in speech. For written language is but a derivative form of speech. Whereas speech signifies the experience of things directly, writing signifies it indirectly, that is, by first signifying speech, which in turn signifies the experience of things. Mc-Luhan's work suggests, however, that this is not quite correct. Although it does appear to be true that speech was developed by man long before writing, this does not mean that writing is but the encoding of speech. Moreover, it does not mean that speech is a more natural form of communication than writing, and writing a more artificial one than speech. It does not mean, above all, that the creation of writing did not affect substantially the nature of speech, or that in the study of the nature of language it is permissible to consider the properties of written "speech" (as linguistic analysts no less than Aristotelian logicians [9] inveterately do) as faithfully reflecting, point for point, the nature of (spoken) speech.

[9] Strangely enough, linguistic analysts, though a recent breed of philosophical traditionalists, are on the whole yet more backward in their assumptions concerning language than contemporary Scholastics, who stand in closer filiation to Aristotelian logic than do the children of British empiricism. Despite the valiant efforts of Ludwig Wittgenstein, P. F. Strawson and a very few others to break through the constrictions of the semantic view of language, linguistic analysts generally not only seem unable to rid themselves of the Aristotelian approach (sometimes they continue to assume a semantic view of language even after having become persuaded that the semantic theory of truth is inadequate), but frequently give the impression

Indeed, the emergence of writing [10] might well be considered but the later stage of development of a single, continuously evolving human phenomenon—let us for the moment continue to call it *communication*—which began with the appearance of speech. Literacy is not added to speech: it transforms speech. That is, literacy alters the nature of human perceptions and affects all modes of human thought (and, hence, speech). Once man is able to read, his language is of a different nature than when he is able to speak only: in this fact, incidentally, we may have a plausible explanation why it was possible, and even historically logical, for Aristotle to misinterpret the nature of language as he did. Let us go back for a moment, the better to understand not only why Aristotle may have thought as he did but, more relevantly to present purposes, in order to appreciate how contemporary scholarship renders his view of the relationship between speech and writing much less obvious than appears at first sight.

One of the key assumptions of the semantic conception of language is that language is articulated out of separate elements: language can be construed as an essentially semantic system, and syntax can be treated as a secondary accretion to language—that

that they try to determine the nature of *human* experience from the way in which *English-speaking* people talk. This is of a piece with the astonishingly provincial fact that a philosophical movement which hinges upon the analysis of language should have so infrequently thought to ask what language is, or to have paid such scant attention to what students of linguistics and allied disciplines have steadily contributed to the subject since long before Bertrand Russell knew how to spell "logical atomism."

[10] I have in mind here, as I will throughout this book, only alphabetic writing. Ideogrammatic and hieroglyphic "writing" have quite different properties, and do not function at all like writing, in our sense of the term. It is indeed only on the basis of Aristotelian semantic presuppositions that the variety of visual languages translatable into speech can be lumped together as "writing."

is, as the mere putting together in complex and elaborate forms the words which are already meaningful before they are put together—only if it is first assumed that a sentence is a linear sequence of discrete elements. McLuhan [11] has convincingly shown the origin of this assumption (and its invalidity concerning speech) in the invention of alphabetic writing (at least, if alphabetic writing is further construed as a semantic system signifying speech rather than as a different sense modality of one and the same linguistic function of the human mind); and he has further explained how this assumption was reinforced and rendered vastly influential in human culture at the dawn of modern times by the invention of typography. For communications technology, which began with the invention of the alphabet, has given man "an eye for an ear." Visually—and, therefore, insofar as it encodes speech —writing is sequential in nature. As *language,* however, insofar as it communicates precisely what one thinks, one would have expected writing to be as involving and enveloping as speech. On the other hand, "the medium is the message." If man begins to speak in a medium which to the eye must appear as a sequence of elements, sooner or later man's speech will lose, at least in part, its enveloping, relational quality. Aristotle thought that words were the signs of mental experience because, if one *looks* at words, that is precisely what they *look* like.

Though McLuhan has been primarily interested in studying how the historical process in question, the shift in the sense modalities of communication, was speeded up through the invention of printing, and how it has been further transformed through the invention of electronic media, the point of particular relevance to this discussion is that the visualization of language, which is

[11] Particularly in *The Gutenberg Galaxy,* (Toronto, 1962).

the direct result of the creation of writing, is the condition of the possibility of the semantic interpretation of language. For the linguistic function of experience became exteriorized, spatialized and stabilized—*scripta manent*—through writing. But because the linguistic function of human consciousness became, once it was written, literally visible and apt to be held off at arm's length, where it could be considered, studied and reflected upon by itself, as a sort of *ex-pression* given off by, or "squeezed out of", the mind, language became detachable from experience itself and could be treated as a surrogate for it. What Aristotle ascribed to speech directly, and to writing only indirectly, namely, the signification of experience (and, therefore, of the reality which is the object of experience), could be ascribed to speech, in truth, only insofar as the invention of writing had permitted the visualization of language (that is, the interpretation of speech on the pattern of script). If the alphabet had never been invented, the semantic concept of language would never have occurred to Aristotle, and the common views that most of us today hold about language would not appear to be nearly as self-evident as we sometimes think.

But this brings us to the sort of difficulty with the Aristotelian view of language which is of decisive importance from the philosophical viewpoint. The semantic idea of language does not only pattern speech on writing; it also patterns thinking, and all manner of mental experience, after speech. Therefore, it ultimately patterns thinking after writing—sequential structure, elemental articulation, and all. For this interpretation, as we have seen, construes speech as a semantic system, that is, as a system of signs which refer the beholder to their corresponding items of mental experience. But this, as we have also seen, implies that mental experience is detachable from the linguistic function and related to it as the inner (and private) is to the external (and public). If so, it follows that *thinking itself* is semantic in nature, that is, it is a mental function which essentially involves signifying—that is, constructing signs for—the realities which are the objects of experience.[12] To be sure, whereas language signifies the reality of one's inner experience for the benefit of another mind, thinking signifies the reality of the outer world for the benefit of one's own mind. In this view, thinking is not merely a signification of reality, but a signification of it to oneself. There are, therefore, important differences between outer speech and inner "speech". But thinking is in any event a sort of speech, that is, it is the production and concatenation of "concepts" or "mental words" (as well as more elaborate signs, like "mental propositions") distinct from, but corresponding to, the spoken words we enunciate whenever we

[12] I should stress, however, that epistemologies of this Aristotelian type do not usually reduce the function of understanding to that of constructing mental signs (concepts, etc.) for reality, but add (as Aristotle himself, in effect, did when he distinguished between the active and the passive intellect) that understanding is the passive qualification of the mind (achieved, however, in the mind's own immanent *act*) by the very perfection of the object of understanding, a passive qualification that is made possible only by the prior activity of signification. Moreover, the mental signs are not what-is-understood, nor is the mental activity of conceptualizing (or making mental propositions and syllogisms) the same as the mental activity of understanding. The signs (mental words at various levels of elaboration) are the *means*—that is, the signifying means—whereby the realities which are the objects of understanding are actually understood. Mental signs, therefore, as later philosophers in this tradition have concluded, do not signify as other signs do, since they are not themselves known before that which they signify, but after. What this really means, however, is that the semantic view of the mind eventually breaks down. For what the foregoing conclusion actually says is that mental signs signify without signifying. Why not say instead that mental signs are not really signs—and that it is necessary, therefore, to attempt to determine anew what understanding may be?

wish not merely to signify reality to ourselves, but further to signify outwardly, usually to another, our inner experience of the world. In brief, the semantic view of language entails a semantic view of consciousness: concepts (and, of course, more elaborate signs) signify reality directly; spoken words (including oral propositions and all manner of discourse) signify concepts, etc., directly and reality indirectly; while written words signify speech directly, concepts indirectly, and reality at yet one more remove.

So far, so good. For the philosopher the difficulty begins, however, when he attempts to study human knowledge on the basis of the foregoing assumptions concerning the semantic nature of thought. For under these assumptions the relationship of the human self to its world can be conceived only in terms of the mind's inward appropriation of the outer world which lies beyond its boundaries. Signification is required by the mind precisely because there is a natural boundary between the self and its world; signs are the means whereby "trans-mission" can occur across the self-delimitation of the mind. Knowledge must be understood as a sort of breaking out of the shell of selfhood in order to reach out (or "in-tend") the objectivity of the real world. More particularly, this out-break, this trans-cending of the self-identity and self-containedness of the mind, is achieved through the mind's signification to itself of the reality of the world. From this it follows in turn that truth, the valuable quality of knowledge, is given to knowledge by the adequation or correspondence of what the mind "says" or signifies to itself, to what in reality is the case.

In other words, from the semantic interpretation of language there ultimately and necessarily follows some variation or another of a semantic epistemology, (that is, a semantic interpretation of knowledge and truth). But the difficulty with every semantic epistemology, as the history of philosophy has demonstrated, is that it leads to self-contradiction. It leads, that is, to the conclusions that knowledge is impossible and that truth is unattainable. Let us examine briefly the outlines of the process that leads to these paradoxes before we consider, in the next chapter, some possible alternative interpretations of the facts.

I may begin by explaining that the classical concept of knowledge which, as I have described it, derives from the classical concept of language, does not reveal its inconsistencies as long as it is coupled with the classical metaphysics, in which the necessary character of reality is consciously assumed. In fact, if one believes, as the Greeks generally did, that necessity or Fate is the true name of reality, then there is no more efficient way of lending to this belief the support of philosophical reason than a theory of knowledge that construes cognition as the mind's inner appropriation of the necessities inherent in things: when thus appropriated by the mind the necessity now becomes the property of the cognizing mind, under the name of *certainty*. And if I appear to insinuate that Greek philosophy enshrined a worshipful attitude towards reality, my intention has been correctly divined. The idea that reality is necessary, and in particular the belief that it exists necessarily—that it could not not exist—is at the very heart of the Greek religious attitude, and the Greek philosophers accepted it without question. Though it is a common impression that Greek philosophy was the antagonist of Greek religion, the fact is that Greek philosophy is rather the supreme expression of the Greek religion. Greek philosophy may well have been iconoclastic and inimical to certain cults and to most of the traditional Greek religious institutions. But it was never anything itself but a profoundly, and often enough even a consciously, religious institution.

52

Christianity, on the other hand, is built upon an attitude towards reality which is at bottom totally incompatible with necessitarianism or fatalism—and, therefore, with Greek philosophy. This attitude is embodied in the belief that God created the world gratuitously, for no reason other than the effusiveness of his goodness, holiness and love. For this, if for no other reason, Christian thought was always more or less at odds with Greek philosophy. Nevertheless, it was not until the time of St. Thomas Aquinas that Christian thought explicitly and with full consciousness recognized that every created being is truly contingent—that is, it need not exist—not simply because it might never have come into being,[13] but above all because its contingency is, as it were, an instrinsic part of its very structure even now, after it has come into being, and even while it continues to exist. And if this contingency belongs to every created being even now that it does exist, it must be apparent in it, and must be demonstrable from man's examination of it, quite apart from every belief that it was created by God.[14]

As I said above, as long as the classical theories of knowledge were coupled with the religious belief that necessity was the true name of reality, the classical theories of knowledge were in principle logically viable: since the reality of the world could be, indeed, had to be, taken for granted (for it was necessary), the appropriation of that reality by means of the mind's signification of it to itself was likewise beyond question or doubt. For these

[13] For instance, because its causes had been rendered inoperative or ineffective.

[14] This is more technically expressed by St. Thomas in the doctrines that (a) in every created being existence is other than essence, and distinct from it, and its act, and (b) we can know an essence without knowing anything about its existence.

53

theories implied that the human mind was essentially infallible in itself—though, to be sure, fallible *per accidens,* fallible insofar as its acquisition of certainty and of the inner necessity of its object might be accidentally impeded by extrinsic reasons (that is, reasons foreign to the nature of the mind itself). But as long as the essential conditions of knowledge were satisfied and knowledge, therefore, actually occurred, *true* knowledge inevitably had to ensue.

After St. Thomas, however, with the recognition of the radical contingency of the world which is the object of human knowledge, the conditions were set that permitted raising the question whether the human mind's acquisition of truth was not intrinsically and by its own nature (rather than extrinsically and by accidental circumstances) every whit as contingent as the reality of the world that was its object. If the world is contingent in itself, can man's knowledge of it ever yield certainty? St. Thomas, in effect—though, as best one can tell, quite unintentionally—destroyed the basis on which had long rested the symbiotic relationship between certainty and truth.

The unbargained-for result of this innovation, however, was the eventual realization by philosophers that knowledge could not be defined in terms of the mind's signification to itself of the reality that lay beyond itself. For after St. Thomas' realization that the contingency of creatures must be grounded in their very inner constitution, in what they are in-and-for-themselves, the conditions were also set for philosophy's eventual conclusion that the classical concept of knowledge did actually assume that the mind was essentially infallible. Therefore, the conditions were also set for the rejection of it. I mean, once philosophy became conscious that the implication of infallibility was indeed contained in classical thought, it could scarcely remain content with it, and was bound eventually to surmount it. For the difficulty with the classical concept of knowledge and its implication of infallibility is not merely that it is hard if not impossible to reconcile with the fact of error, but above all that it shows up that concept of knowledge as self-contradictory and paradoxical.

For if human knowledge is indeed infallible, but its object is contingent, there can be no way of testing the difference—that is, no way of *knowing* the difference—between an act of knowledge which truly signified a real object, and one which signified it erroneously (or, indeed, one which did not signify it *at all*). That is, if knowledge is deemed infallible, but the existence of its object cannot be put in doubt (because it is necessary), the essential infallibility of human knowledge may seem strange, and even difficult to uphold in view of the apparent fact of error, but is not self-contradictory: this was the bliss of Greek philosophy from beginning to end. But if knowledge is deemed to be infallible, at the same time that the existence of worldly objects is held to be contingent (and, therefore, not guaranteed either by the nature of such worldly objects, nor by our knowledge of them, for our knowledge being but our signification of them to ourselves requires the *prior* existence of such objects in order to take place), it follows that there is no detectable (that is, *knowable*) difference between true knowledge and error: this was the plight of Christian thought after St. Thomas up to recent times.[15]

Of course— but we can say *of course* only in retrospect—the real

[15] It is still the plight of some philosophical circles even today. Most philosophers in the secular tradition of the English-speaking world remain puzzled by the problems first raised by Descartes, Locke, Berkeley and Hume. It is possible, therefore, that their next step may be to discover the work of Kant and Hegel.

lesson to be learned from the protracted historical episode I have so cavalierly described above was that the classical concept of knowledge was thoroughly inadequate. And it was inadequate in the first place because it was understood on the analogy of linguistic signification. Just as the semantic idea of language implied so deep a chasm between language and thought that no body-soul theory could span it, the corresponding theories of knowledge implied so radical a separation between the mind and reality that no amount of knowledge could possibly overcome it. Hence, the supreme paradox of the classical epistemologies: the very existence of objects of actual knowledge could be put in doubt.

This is self-contradictory, because it supposes that one might not know what one does know. It is not only common sense that asserts the obvious truth that, however radically contingent, the world of objects does in fact exist. For the mind knows enough *about itself* to know that it is other than the non-self, other than the world. Nevertheless, it is a fact of the history of philosophy that if we proceed to define knowledge on the assumptions made by the Greek philosophers concerning the nature of language, it turns out that the facts which are not only well attested to by common sense, but even presupposed by philosophy, namely, (a) that we do know, and (b) that the world exists, become, upon reflection, philosophically problematic. Small wonder that in not a few circles philosophy in modern times has earned rather a bad name for itself.

If knowledge is the mind's signification of objects to itself, then knowledge is the mind's overcoming of its isolation from the world. But what could possibly provide the ground on which this overcoming could effectively occur, if the isolation of the mind from its world were not merely a physical or spatial one, but pertained to the order of its very reality and being? For, as was fully realized for the first time in the history of philosophy only by St. Thomas Aquinas, the classical concept of knowledge makes sense only if what separates the knowing subject from the world of objects, and is thereafter overcome by knowledge, (and, moreover, only if what distinguishes the act of signification from that which is signified and is thereafter rejoined by thought), is the uniqueness of the act of existing by which the mind and its object are each rendered themselves, mind and object, precisely as actual and real. But this is the very ground of scepticism. If object and subject were isolated by anything less radical than their very existential reality as actual beings, their mutual isolation would be less than absolute and could be, at least in principle, overcome. If, on the contrary, what isolates subject from object is existence itself (that is, the existence of the subject no less so than the existence of the object), then each existent, no matter how powerful its capacity for knowing or being known might be, is cut off from every other existent, precisely because it exists and because the other exists.

To sum up: to say that knowledge is the mind's transcending of that which cannot be transcended as long as it exists, and even as long as the mind exists, is to say that knowledge is the overcoming of the sort of isolation between knower and known which cannot be overcome at all. The upshot of adopting a concept of knowledge that makes the mind infallible is, paradoxically, the conclusion that there can be no knowledge at all—not even erroneous knowledge. Evidently, a concept of knowledge that leads to this conclusion begs for re-examination at the root.

Nor is this the end of the vicissitudes of epistemology since St. Thomas. For just as the semantic concept of language implies a semantic concept of knowledge, so the semantic concept of knowledge implies a semantic concept of truth—the problems and paradoxes of which are at least as serious as those of its antecedent view of language and thought.

If language is the outward signification of experience, experience is the mind's inner self-signification of reality. True knowledge is, therefore, true signification of reality. Truth is a quality that accrues to knowledge insofar as knowledge is significant of reality, that is, insofar as knowledge consists in signifying or telling ourselves what reality is like. To tell the truth is, of course, to express outwardly (to another) a sign which does actually signify what we in fact have in mind; and to tell a falsity (or a lie, if we do so willfully) is, as everyone in this tradition knows, to utter signs which do not in point of fact signify what we actually think, or know, to be true.

As to willful falsity, no problem arises: lying may be reprehensible, but does not rend the fabric of epistemology. But as to the other instance, it must be said that what we think to be true *is* true if our thinking actually "says" (to ourselves) what in point of fact the signified object in reality actually is. The truth of knowledge is, therefore, in every respect like the truth of speech. That is, truth is a semantic relation of correspondence or adequation between the signification of the mind (to itself) and what is signified. The only difference is, of course, that speech can be mendacious as well as erroneous, whereas knowledge can be erroneous only, since no one can actually think that what he thinks to be true is actually false, or vice versa. But this is precisely what brings up one of the key difficulties of the semantic concept of truth: if knowledge is the mind's self-signification of reality, and if no one can think that what he thinks to be true is in reality false, how can there possibly be any erroneous knowledge? How can there be a mistaken apprehension of reality (that is, an apprehension of it which does not conform to it), if knowledge is the mind's apprehension, for itself, of the reality that outside the mind exists in-and-for-itself? Would it not rather seem that all knowledge that is truly knowledge must be true, and that erroneous knowledge is not really knowledge at all?

It is easy to see how there can be mendacious speech. And it is not impossible to understand how there can be erroneous *speech:* one might well intend to say that "A is B," but one's tongue, what with neurophysiological processes and the like, might become twisted, as we say, so that one will actually say the opposite, all the time thinking however that one *has* said "A is B." (And if one hears oneself say otherwise one will immediately remedy one's trivial mishap.) But what of erroneous *knowledge?* Could it be said that it is something of the same order? If there are slips of the tongue, and even slips of the pen, why could there not be slips of the mind?

If so, it should be said that erroneous knowledge occurs when some extrinsic factor intervenes in the process of self-signification, so that one's signification will actually signify the opposite of— what? Surely not the opposite of what one thinks. As we saw earlier, one could *say,* whether willfully or accidentally, the opposite of what one *thought.* But one cannot very well say, either willfully or accidentally, the opposite of what one says. Likewise, one cannot *think* the opposite of what one *thinks.* I repeat, one cannot do this either willfully or accidentally, because the very supposition is self-contradictory. Could we perhaps say, then, that error is the accidental intervention in the process of self-signification of an extraneous factor which so vitiates the mind's self-signification of reality that it will actually signify to itself the opposite of what in reality is the case?

The difficulty with this is that, according to the classical concept of knowledge, we only know what in reality is the case *by means of what we think about it:* this is of the very essence of conceiving knowledge as the mind's *signification* of reality to itself. The semantic view of knowledge converts thinking into a *means* to knowledge; it makes thinking an intermediary between reality and the self. If so, the mind's self-signification of reality could signify to itself the opposite of what in reality is the case only by signifying to itself the opposite of what it in fact signifies to itself. We thus arrive, more circuitously but as surely, at exactly the same paradox as before.

Maybe we should try one last, rocky detour. Could we say that error *does* really consist in thinking the opposite of what in reality is the case, precisely because some extraneous factor so deranges thought that thought becomes self-contradictory? Could we say, in effect, that error does consist in thinking the opposite of what one thinks?

Well, in a way this must be granted to be true. That is, it becomes the definition of error in the light of the classical view of knowledge. On the assumption that truth is the conformity of the mind to reality as the mind says of what is that it is, or of what is not that it is not, it *does* follow that error is the dis-conformity of the mind to reality, as it says of what is not that it is, or of what is that it is not. But it could scarcely be thought that this does away with the impossibility of thinking what one does not think— not to mention *not* thinking what one *does* think. Or that one has explained anything at all when one has explained that error lies in the fact that the mind mistakes what is for what is not, and vice versa. For all one has done is to reason circularly: the explanation of error lies in the fact that mistakes are made. Thus, the correspondence concept of truth, quite in accordance with the concept of knowledge which is its close correlate, actually assumes that the human mind is infallible. Indeed, it is because the mind is infallible that making an error must consist in achieving the impossible feat of thinking the opposite of what one thinks. The mildest construction that can be put upon this absurdity is that the semantic concept of knowledge, quite as noted at the outset, assumes that erroneous knowledge is not truly knowledge. Error, it says, is no knowledge at all. Conversely, real knowledge is necessarily true. Or, if I may so put it, knowledge that is truly knowledge is necessarily true knowledge, whereas knowledge that is false is not truly knowledge of any sort. It may have the appearance of knowledge, but is not knowledge at all—for only true knowledge is really true.

At first sight this may appear, though perhaps a trifle eccentric, not a particularly dangerous conclusion. Despite the real mistakes that men do seem to make, it might not be too difficult to believe that the human mind is essentially infallible, if only we made careful allowance for the mind's "accidental" mistakes due to factors foreign to the cognitive faculties and processes. On second thought, however, we may discover (as the history of philosophy eventually did discover) that an essentially infallible human mind is a lesser asset than one might have initially believed. For, as we have seen, false knowledge is falsely knowledge: it may have the appearance of knowledge, but it is neither true knowledge nor even truly knowledge at all. Yet, to repeat, it *appears* to be knowledge. Well, if false knowledge, despite its being false knowledge, and despite its being no knowledge at all, nevertheless has the appearance of knowledge, how could anyone ever tell, how could anyone ever distinguish, how could anyone ever *know,* the difference between truth and error? The only answer is: no one could tell, no one could find out, no one could possibly know. The only reasonable outcome of infallibilism is scepticism.

I say the only *reasonable* one, for an unreasonable possibility also exists. And since philosophers, though almost universally logical, are not infrequently quite unreasonable, the answer that in point of fact has been given to this question by many schools of philosophy has not been scepticism, but dogmatism. If it is held that the mind is essentially infallible, and only accidentally subject to error, it will not be every philosopher who will resist the temptation to account for every difference of opinion by using the apparent truth of his own thinking as the criterion whereby to judge the truth and falsity of the thinking of others. Indeed, on the continued assumption of the classical epistemologies the only alternative to so doing would be, as I said, scepticism. And, to be sure, scepticism may hold the moral edge over dogmatism and intolerance. But it is scarcely a solution to the problem of knowledge, and philosophers have never rested satisfied with it.

What has become increasingly clear in modern times—though unfortunately it is still far from clear to not a few—is that the antinomies of scepticism and dogmatism are unavoidable once the traditional assumptions of our epistemological heritage are granted. Thus, the reconstruction of our philosophical tradition must reach back to the interpretation of language which undergirds it and supports it as a matter of historical fact. What sort of alternative suggests itself when we do reach back to the interpretation of language against the background of criticism sketched in these lectures so far? This is the question to which our attention shall now be turned.

62

3.

Truth and Reality

No one who has had the opportunity to read a transcript of the recording of a spontaneous, real-life conversation in which he has participated will have failed to experience the startingly vast difference between spoken language and written language. A perfectly intelligible, flowing and seemingly logical dialogue becomes a halting, meaningless jumble of half-finished sentences, false starts and non-sequiturs which would not be tolerated in the prose of a ten-year old. No one who has had first-hand acquaintance with both speech and writing as creative media, whether poetry or prose, drama or novel, scholarly enquiry or literary criticism, would be easily tempted to treat speech as unwritten language, or writing as transcribed speech. Fluency in one of these media does not entail skill in the other. Both speech and writing may come under the heading of communication; but they are, as media, as different from each other as an ideogram is from a word—or, as McLuhan has pointed out, as different as the telephone is from television. The facility with which we can, more or less approximately, translate from one to the other, and back, blinds us to the fact that in reality every translation is always a new message. Not, to be sure, necessarily a totally different message, but truly a new one nonetheless.

Traduttore, traditore: this is, in a way, a correct observation, but a little unfair to translators. A *mere* translation cannot but betray

63

the original—rather, in order not to betray the original a translation has to be more than a translation. It has to be a re-writing of it. This is true also in the case of "translating" from speech to script. (Incidentally, it is also true in the opposite case, translating from writing to speech. It requires special skills—for instance, the actor's—to read writing aloud without traducing the original.)

Linguistic equivalence is not the same as logical—least of all mathematical—equality. The flow of speech has a Heraclitean quality. One can never swim in the same stream of speech twice. One can never speak the same words a second time. This is but one way in which speech, unlike writing, exhibits close kinship with thought. Speech, like thought, scarcely resembles the measured logic, the linear sequence, the articulate composition, of writing. Though we cannot very well criticize Aristotle for having thought that writing was to speech as speech was to thought— for it is difficult to think of any historically likely reason why he should have realized that it is not—we could hardly be said to have profited from the vast accumulation of human experience (made possible indeed by no more faithful memory and no more efficient technique than by script and typography), if we today were to do no better than Aristotle did.

It may be difficult, of course, to attempt to study language in abstraction from every visual consideration, putting aside all that we tend to ascribe to it because of what we have learned from the supposed equivalence of the media of writing and speech. That is, it may be difficult for us today, who are literate, to study language keeping in mind but the phenomenon of *speech,* prescinding from every idea that derives from the semantic interpretation of it which has been constantly dinned into our ears—rather, constantly presented to our eyes—for two and a half thousand years by the not-so-implicit connotations of our everyday linguistic life. If we succeed, however, in taking this fresh look at language— rather, if we succeed in listening to it as if for the first time—we are apt to see language in a new light. Or perhaps I should say, we are apt to hear its sound with new overtones. For if we consider linguistic behaviour anew, without presupposing a semantic interpretation of it, or any of the elements of such an interpretation, we are apt to discover two things about it. (As it so happens, at this point we can best express them negatively, in relation to the Aristotelian view, but their negativity does not lessen their importance.) They are, first, that words are not signs; they are neither the signs of the experience or reality, nor of reality itself. Second, there is no empirically detectable difference between speaking and thinking.

These two observations are intimately connected; we may begin with the second, which is actually, in a way, the antecedent of the first. The assertion that there is no detectable difference between speaking and thinking may appear at first sight as obviously incorrect and perhaps even preposterous. For it would seem to be a matter of common experience that one can do a great deal of thinking without making the slightest vocal utterance or other sound. One can easily think "Just you wait, 'enry 'iggins, just you wait!" or "Wouldn't it be lovely to spend a holiday with Miss Doolittle in Spain?" without actually uttering a threat that one's mentor could hear, or without revealing one's reveries to one's ward. But what this actually means is that one can think without vocalizing one's thought—a matter on which I for one would not wish to cast any doubt. What I would contend is that this human ability to think without vocalizing is in effect the ability to *speak* without vocalization.

The expression "to speak without vocalization" may appear at first a little forced. I have used it on the analogy of well-sanctioned terms used in phonetics, where a distinction is drawn between "voiced" and "voiceless" vocal sounds.[1] But perhaps it would be better to use these very phonetic terms. I would then say that thought is actually voiceless speech. Or I might put it the other way about and say that speech is really voiced thought, or that voicing alone, without thought—if this is possible—is no speech at all. A tape recorder, as I suggested in the previous chapter, does not speak; it reproduces vocal sounds. If I send you a message on tape it is I who *speaks* to you when you listen to the vocal sounds reproduced by the machine.

What is the evidence supporting the view that thought is voiceless speech, and speech voiced thought? It is that although the relationship in which I place myself towards a *listener* is different when I "think" than when I "speak," the relationship in which I place myself towards the *reality* of which I speak or think is no different when I "think" than when I "speak." This assumes, of course, a non-Aristotelian viewpoint: it assumes that linguistic behaviour is not pure and simply communication to another, and that the more adequate viewpoint from which to analyze the phenomenon of speech is that of the speaker, not that of the listener. It assumes, in other words, that *speech is first of all and essentially what I say, and only secondarily what you hear*. It is from this viewpoint that, as I suggest, there is no difference, other than voicedness or voicelessness, between thought and speech.

For example, even when the speaker is a professional phonologist and grammarian, in what pertains to his relationship to the

[1] For instance, the *s* in "rose" is voiced; the *s* in "snapdragon" is voiceless.

66

reality it makes no difference whether he "merely" thinks about sunny Spain, possibly with anticipation, or whether he says anything about it, beginning to lay his plans. Of course, it does decidedly make a difference to Eliza whether Henry merely thinks about lechery on the Castilian plain, or whether he actually proposes a week-end in a *parador*. But is the philandering philologist's thinking it anything other than his saying it to himself? Or could he *say* to her what he thinks, without thinking it, without saying it to himself? There is, to repeat, a clear and important difference between thinking and thinking out loud, between speaking and speaking to oneself, between "mere" thought and voiced thought. This is why, as I said, speech cannot be adequately understood as nothing but a means of communication—hence, it is not essentially semantic in nature—though it can undoubtedly serve in that role. But there is no thinking anterior to, or behind, speech—though, of course, I can "think it over," that is, say it to myself, before I communicate to another what I think. For to say it I must think it, and to think it I must say it. It is impossible to detect empirically any real difference between the two.

But, this much having been granted, it may seem as if I have proven nothing at all. For is not the Aristotelian idea precisely that thinking is signified by certain (voiced) sounds? Yes, to be sure, but what I have tried to show is *not* that the inner function of thinking having been accomplished, there is no need to speak unless one wants to communicate one's thought, in which case one's thought is spoken, that is, signified by means of vocal sounds. This, I repeat, is *not* what I have concluded above. What I believe I have given some evidence for is the view that thinking is not an inner function, but that it is accomplished only in speech—though speech may in turn be voiced or not—and that, beyond this, provided that speech is voiced, thought may be communicated to another mind. Thus, I have tried to show that the distinction which is in fact displayed by linguistic behavior is not between thinking and the voiced sounds that signify thinking, but between (voiceless) thinking and voiced thought.

The fact appears to be that with but a little training human beings can do their thinking tacitly and not merely in its more basic vocal form. This fact does not mean, however, that speech is a function separate or distinct from thought, nor, therefore, that speech signifies thought. By the same token, speech cannot be reduced to communication: to *speak to* it is necessary first to *speak,* that is, to think. To speak to Eliza is not to translate one's thinking into voiced sounds, but to voice one's thinking and, moreover, to voice one's thinking *to* (or towards) her. On the other hand, because to *speak to* one must first speak, one cannot *speak to* without oneself thinking what one says. There is no distinction between speaking and thinking, though there is a distinction between *saying* and *telling.* What does Henry do when he *says* "It's raining outside, so we'll have to stay in," that he does not do when he *thinks* "It's raining outside, so we'll have to stay in"—except, of course, *telling* Eliza (possibly in more ways than one) precisely what he is thinking?

If you know what I say, do you not know what I think? If I am a deceiver, you may not know, of course, that what I *told* you is not at all what I think; it may not even be what I believe. But to tell someone even what one does not believe one has to think it and *say* it. That is, to think it, even if one does not believe it, one has to say it to oneself. For, as I have already suggested twice before, speech is not parrotting. It is not even parrotting one's own thought. A tape recorder does not speak: *it* signifies the speech of the mind that spoke into it. And it is indeed the *mind,* the *thinking* mind, that speaks, not the vocal chords and the rest of the linguistic apparatus (which ultimately comprises up to cortical and other areas of the brain). On the other hand, the mind usually speaks with—rather, it speaks *in*—the entire vocal apparatus. This is why thinking is not an "inner" phenomenon that goes on somewhere behind the human body in a non-corporeal reality called the mind: the mind (at least in my usage of the term) is but the human body's consciousness of itself. On the other hand, the mind can learn to speak only with part of the vocal apparatus, as when it merely imagines, without vocally producing, the voicing of thought. In brief, by reducing speech to communication, Aristotle reduced speech to vocalization: this is the essence of the semantic view. Unfortunately, this severed thought from speech—rather, it reduced vocalization to signification (which is "outer"), while reducing the linguistic function, speech, (which is in reality other than signification), to thought (which is "inner"). Or, conversely, it misinterpreted the nature of thought by confining it to the "inner" world of the mind, and by taking away from it one of its truly essential features, namely, its linguistic form. Modern linguists have not radically departed from this merely because, for instance, they have reduced the essence of language to the *inner* signification of a signified concept, achieved by an acoustic image rather than by an actual sound (de Saussure), or because they have distinguished between the "content-form" and the "content-substance" (Hjelmslev), or between the "deep structure" and the "surface structure" of the sentence (Chomsky). For these interpretations still reduce the essential function of language to the signification of a signified—a signified which would remain logically prior to every linguistic structure or form or act.

Here we touch upon the fundamental issue: *is thought, as the semantic understanding of language assumes, essentially prior to language?* That is, does language *express* thought? (For chronological priority, I stress, is not in question.) Is a linguistic form, therefore, (whatever its nature might be), somehow *given to* an essentially prior thought-matter or experience content? Or, on the contrary, is the linguistic form not *discerned in* the original reality of human linguistic thought—quite like the mental content, which, as distinct from the linguistic form, is but an abstraction drawn from the prior reality, namely, the aboriginal linguistic consciousness or spoken-thought which defines actual human experience?

For, in order to divorce thought from its linguistic form, the semantic view of language has to suppose the priority (if not of time at least of nature) of thought over speech. However, this supposition is rebutted not only by the fact I have already mentioned, namely, that there is no thought which does not consist of the same "words" as the speech that corresponds to it, but also by the consideration that the "words" of thought are *in the first place* spoken words. When a child learns to speak he does not learn to translate that which he already knows how to think, into his mother-tongue, say, English. To learn to think it in English is to learn to *think* it—unless, of course, one already knows how to think it *in another language*. The point is that one cannot think it except in some given language. To learn one's mother-tongue is to learn to think in one's mother-tongue. Likewise, to learn to think is to learn to think in one's mother-tongue, say, English—or else, of course, in French, Swahili, or some other given tongue.

The last point is important—and the source of much confusion. One can only think in some given tongue, but one need not think in any given tongue rather than another. This implies the very opposite of Aristotle's opinion that "the mental experiences which [words] directly signify are the same for all [men]." It implies, that is, that the "mental experience" of one and the same worldly reality varies from man to man—and specially from culture to cuture, since it is only among cultures rather than among individuals within the same culture that linguistic differences are profound—precisely because the linguistic form of human thought varies among men.

Moreover, the contingency of the morphology of languages, the fact that among the specifically different ways of saying things in the various human languages none can claim to be the only "right" one, and none can be completely "wrong," [2] facilitates the Aristotelian misinterpretation of the nature of language. It is easy to imagine that, since one does not have to think in any one given language, it is not necessary, indeed it is impossible, to think in any language—though it is admitted that one's non-linguistic thought can be *outwardly signified* only in some given language or another. And the semantic misinterpretation of the nature of language is unfortunately further reinforced by the fact that once one knows how to speak, one will most likely begin to learn a second language by translating one's thinking (in one's first language) into the words of the second language—which one will thus, in fact, use as signs of one's own mother-tongue. Of course, to the extent that one's knowledge of a second language remains at this level, one will lack facility and fluency in that language. Finally,

[2] There can be, on the other hand, more or less adequate languages in relation to given purposes. For speaking about the Arctic weather the richness of the various Eskimo dialects is proverbial. For philosophizing in the Scholastic manner Latin is unsurpassed. For viewing the world scientifically the modern European languages are especially apt.

71

the same misinterpretation of the nature of language receives additional dubious corroboration from the observation that after we know how to speak (and, therefore, how to think) we *can,* albeit to a limited extent, use words as signs. Name-calling is a good instance of this. The extension of one's vocabulary through the unreliable procedure of learning synonyms is another. But it is significant that this is unreliable and of very limited value: even with the aid of the best dictionaries (that is, dictionaries that try to explain the function of a word rather than its supposed signification) one does not necessarily know quite how to use a word adequately simply because one has learned what it "means." The awkward performance of the educational *nouveau riche* frequently illustrates the sort of thing I mean.

Thus, language can scarcely be construed as the signification of thought since, in a sense, speech is prior to thought—I mean, the linguistic form of thinking is what makes every human thought to be concretely and precisely the thought it is. I would not want to stress this priority, since there is, in my suggestion, no real distinction between the two, anyway. The point is that it would be less misleading to speak of the priority of speech over thought than the other way about. For instance, the theory that thought is the signification of speech to oneself (and I have myself used this sort of expression above) or, if you wish, the theory that consciousness is the result of man's ability to "express" his own speech to himself in a voiceless, private and "interior" fashion—this theory, I say, might well need some refinement and precision before it coordinates well the multiplicity of relevant observations. (I would be particularly doubtful whether such "signification" could be properly so-called.[3]) But, at any rate, it would be much closer to

---

[3] In fact, it would be better called *symbolization.* For the distinction between *sign* and *symbol* see *Foundations of Belief,* pp. 93–94.

the truth than the opposite, Aristotelian construction, in terms of a semantic correspondence of speech to thought.

Now, speech need not be prior to thought in every respect, and particularly not in a temporal sense. In fact, if there is no distinction between speech and thought, as I have repeatedly suggested, but only between voiced and voiceless thought (or, which is the same, between speech and vocalization, or between linguistic function and vocal function), so that there is no distinction between, for instance, learning to speak and learning to speak a specific language, (even if to learn to speak or think one must learn to do so in *some* language), then it follows that speech cannot be formally speaking prior to thought; at least not in the sense that there could be linguistic form without thinking activity. The priority in question is in the first place causal or, rather, genetic. Man is not a speaking animal because he is a thinking one; man can think only because he can speak. For if we suppose that man is the creature of some evolutionary process, it would seem likely that man did *not* acquire linguistic skills on the basis provided by the prior development, however rudimentary, of the ability to think. On the contrary, he must have developed cogitative skills, and even consciousness, because he evolved biologically into a speaking animal—that is, an animal that could use its body, particularly though by no means exclusively his neurophonetic apparatus, to think. Let us say: language is the condition of the possibility of thought. Thus, the priority of language over thought also refers to the fact that after one learns to think vocally one may further develop, (presumably through some neurophysiological process) one's ability to think by learning to think voicelessly, (that is, by merely imagining conceptually what one previously could think only vocally). But this is another way of saying that thinking and speaking are not really distinct, though there may be different modes of thinking—or, which is the same, of speaking. The Aristotelian understanding of language takes advantage of the distinction between these degrees or forms of speech (that is, thought), and misconceptualizes it as a distinction between thought (the self-signification of reality) and speech (the other-signification of thought). Once this mistake is made, the entire semantic theory of language becomes unavoidable. For, finally, the priority of speech over thought also refers to the fact that *after we speak* (that is, after we think linguistically) it is possible by reflection, given the self-present character of human consciousness, to abstract the thought-content from the linguistic form (or, of course, the linguistic form from the thought-content). But if, when we do this, we fail to observe that this dichotomy between thought and speech is the result of the reflexive properties of human consciousness (that is, properties which follow upon its self-present character), then we will naturally and unavoidably assume that thought and speech are distinct in themselves—from which we will in turn be naturally and unavoidably led to the idea that thought is essentially prior to speech, and speech the subsequent expression of thought. Conversely, once we avoid mistaking the difference between voiced and voiceless thought for a real distinction between thought and speech, the semantic view of language ceases to exert its fascination and loosens its hold upon us.

More precisely, it becomes superfluous and even untenable. If there is no dichotomy between thought and speech, there can be no question about their relationship. There can be no room for asking the question: If language is not the verbal semantic system that translates the mental semantic system from the spiritual realm of inner individuality to the physical realm of the outer world, how does language, then, express our thinking of reality? There are legitimate questions to be raised at this point, but the foregoing is not one of them. What we might well ask is, rather: What is language, if it is not the expression of thought or the outward signification of our inner experience of reality? How shall we interpret linguistic behaviour, once we reject the semantic construction put upon it since Aristotelian times?

Well, perhaps a useful way of stating the view of language which is implicit in the results of our enquiry so far might be the following: rather than the *reflection* of our mental relationship to reality, language is the *construction* or *creation* of such a relationship. And let us in turn symbolize this interpretation in more explicit form in this other formula: the linguistic function that defines speech is not essentially *semantic,* but *syntactic,* so that, correspondingly, words are not signs, but symbols (that is, functions embodying and concretizing man's selfhood, consciousness and creativity) of man's mental relationship to the world.

Perhaps I can best illustrate what I have in mind when I distinguish between the structural and the functional, the semantic and the syntactic, ways of understanding language, by means of an analogy drawn from my own experience. I have very little musical ability, and what little I do possess has never been developed. Nevertheless, I once learned to play "God save the Queen" on the piano, index-finger style. Now, I was taught to play it, as it so happens, in the key of C (for the very simple reason that it was the easiest—no black keys). And I had picked up somewhere the information that the scale consists of seven notes (which I could actually hum passably well), which repeated themselves beginning at the octave. But my musical education having been halted at this point, I spontaneously developed a *semantic* concept of music. That is, I conceived the idea that a melody was composed of a sequence of different sounds, each of which was signified by a note which, in turn, was produced by the corresponding piano key. I thought, in other words, that the first two notes of "God save the Queen," *do do,* were invariably "signified" and produced by the key of C, that the third note, *re,* corresponded to and was struck invariably by the key of D, and so on.

I knew, of course, that the same melody could be played higher or lower, that "God save the Queen" could begin with either middle C, high C, or the octave above high C—just as the sound "table", which signifies certain pieces of furniture, can be translated into *Tisch* or into *wei*. It was with not a little sense of pleasant astonishment that, years later, I discovered the truth that "God save the Queen" could be played beginning with any key of the piano, and that the notes *do do re* may be as aptly produced by the keys C C D, as by D D E, as indeed by E E F♯, by B♭ B♭ C, and so on. My great discovery, of course, was no more than what every child of but mediocre musical talent learns at a tender age: that to play a melody on the piano is not to produce a certain sequence of specific sounds which correspond to the elements of a certain fixed musical structure, but that it is to produce a certain pattern of sounds, a pattern which can be aptly described only in terms of the function performed by the relationship among the sounds. This *function* is precisely what is called music; and musical "language" is not a semantic but a syntactic system. The notes do not *stand* for specific "notified" elements, the structural combination of which constitutes a melody; they function com-positionally to *make* music.

On the other hand, what many people who understand the

elements of music very well cannot readily comprehend is that language, like music, is not a structural-semantic system, but a functional-syntactic one. To distinguish between thought and language makes as little sense as distinguishing between the music we hear and the *musical* sounds produced by the piano. There can be sounds which do not make music, but musical sounds are musical precisely as sounds. The music we hear is the music of the musical sounds. One cannot make musical sounds by matching, however skillfully, music and sounds—or language by matching, however closely, thought and voice. On the other hand, we may easily distinguish between music and sound—or between linguistic thought and vocalization. A piano can be muted; its sound can be muffled, and perhaps even suppressed. There is a distinction between music and striking the piano keys. This does not take away the fact that it is the musical sound itself that is musical, and that music is musical sound—even when we "hear" it or play it only in the silence of our own creative (or imitative) imagination within.

Against the background of the syntactic conception of language, and having left behind the illegitimate question "How does language express the experience of reality?" we may profitably ask any of the numberless philosophical questions that linguists, psychologists, anthropologists and phonologists commonly ask concerning the nature of linguistic behaviour—including, for instance, questions about the development of voiceless out of voiced thought. We may well also ask the questions that philosophers are more likely to be interested in. For instance: What does the essential identity of the linguistic and the cogitative functions tell us about the nature of thinking, of consciousness and of man? What does it imply for an understanding of man's relationship to

77

reality? And what is the meaning of the discrepancy, which for all its deficiencies the semantic view of language did at least dispose of, namely, the discrepancy between the variability of the words (*Tisch, mensa, wei*) of different languages, and the invariability of "this table," the reality to which speech must in some way or another (that is, by way of signification or otherwise) ultimately refer?

As we saw in the previous chapter, the semantic interpretation of the nature of language logically implies a semantic concept of knowledge and a semantic concept of truth. The resolution of the dichotomy between thought and speech is the dissolution of its epistemological implications. But what is to replace them? What are the corresponding implications of its alternative? Though the detailed and fully demonstrative answer to these questions is neither simple nor brief, the gist of it can be put in a few words. It is the view that talking about reality makes it meaningful to us. For thinking about reality, and knowing and understanding it, is not to acquire its perfection vicariously, nor to reduplicate within ourselves the meaning that it contains within itself. Thinking "about" reality is not really thinking *about* it, or thinking *of* it, but thinking *towards* it and thinking *at* it. It is to project ourselves *into* it—and, thus, to find ourselves *in* it. For this self-projection into it is what in turn constitutes human nature into a self. Well, how does this way of understanding the basic nature of the mind's relationship to reality correlate with the concept of language sketched above?

When we think "about" the world—that is, when we speak it—we enter into a *new* relationship with it. But if this is a new relationship, the reason is that there was an old one to begin with: this is the relationship that anything in the world, even if it does not think, has to everything else in the world. But this is a sort of passive relationship: it does not consist in *relating to,* but in *being related to* (for instance, being close or far, being like or unlike, being better or worse, being a cause or an effect, and so on). To think or talk about the world, however, is to create a relationship to it; man is not merely related to, but *self-related* to, the world. Thinking is one's becoming related to the world precisely as a self, that is, as that which is not only related to it but knows its relations to it. So, when I am conscious of the table I exist, as it were, "in" the table—or, perhaps better, *at* the table. But I exist there as a self; my existing at the table does not confuse me with the table. On the contrary, I exist at the table only as other-than-it. Hence, it is by one and the same function that I am conscious of the world and that I am conscious of myself. To be conscious of myself I must be conscious of the table, and vice versa. Thus, my talking about the world is the means of my becoming conscious of myself as a self, that is, as a being who relates itself, precisely as a self, to the world.

Since neither language nor thought have a significant (I mean, a signifying) function, and since neither is significative of reality, the truth of language and thinking cannot be their correspondence or conformity with (or any other form of replication of) reality. What language and thought achieve is the creation, the viability, the facilitation and the continuation of the emergence of human selfhood in relation to the world. Now, if I am going to think "correctly" towards reality, I must, of course *abide by* the world as it actually is; I must respect, and faithfully deal with, the real state of affairs. But abiding by reality, faithfully dealing with it, and even respecting it, do not imply reproducing it, or representing it or, in however analogous a matter, uniting or unifying oneself with it, or possessing it, or acquiring its perfection. On the contrary, such expressions as abiding by reality, respecting its factuality and dealing with it as it actually is, should convey above all what *we* do and what happens to *us*—rather, what we make happen to us—and not anything that happens to reality.

No doubt, once we talk about reality, or think it, we may, reflecting upon the matter, compare the truth of our consciousness with the reality of which the truth is the abiding-by. If so, there will be a correspondence of mind and reality—or, perhaps, absence of correspondence, in the case of thinking which lacks truth. What this means, of course, is that *true* knowledge actually does, indeed must, correspond to reality. It corresponds to reality, however, precisely *because* it is true. To suppose that truth *is* such correspondence, or worse yet, that the correspondence is the cause of truth, would be to suffer from the understandable but abysmal confusion attendant upon the semantic interpretation of language and truth. And may I remark in passing that the difference between saying that true knowledge does correspond to reality and conforms to it precisely because it is true, and saying, on the contrary, that knowledge is true if, when, or because it corresponds to reality or conforms to it, is far from a subtlety of mere academic significance. For the semantic understanding of truth, as I previously suggested, is the basis of the justification of dogmatism—if not also a temptation to it. Truth must be so understood as to leave open the possibility that some knowledge that is truly knowledge may be truly in error.

Some people who find themselves in apparent general agreement with the foregoing line of thought have been known, however, to introduce at this point a distinction between two kinds of truth. They may allege that the sort of argument which I have thus far illustrated is correct insofar as it may apply to the world of moral, spiritual, religious, artistic or poetic human existence. But they may cavil at the supposition that it might be proposed also in relation to the physical world itself—for instance, to the world that the scientist and the physician deal with, the world of plain, hard fact. It may well be, they say, that from the viewpoint of ethics, which has to do with the future, or from the viewpoint of theology, or art, or feeling, or emotion, or perhaps more broadly, from the viewpoint of human creative existence, truth is that quality of the development of consciousness which leads to its further self-development, a quality which is given by the orientation of consciousness in the direction that leads beyond itself—for instance, beyond that which it already knows. But in more mundane matters and in everyday, practical, present and immediate life, truth must be recognized for the simple relationship which tradition has always said it was. For the facts are the facts. Either it is raining outside or it is not; and either we think that it is, or else that it is not. What is wrong with admitting that at least on the level of factual existence truth *is* the conformity of mind to the actual state of affairs?

If human knowledge were, even in some elementary respects, the mind's signification of reality to itself, the answer would be: nothing. If truth in all its forms and in all its guises, however, must be understood as the typical value of the projective character of human consciousness, the reason is that cognition, in the first place, in all its forms and in all its guises must be understood as having such projective character. And this must be maintained as long as it is deemed that language is not, *at any level,* semantic in nature. That is, the language of the scientist is not semantic in nature; nor is that of the physician, the car mechanic, the plumber or the housewife.

Allow me to repeat: if some types of levels of language were semantic, the truth corresponding to such types or levels of knowledge would be likewise semantic in nature. But if the view of language presented above is true of all language, even of the language of everyday, practical life and of hard, obstinate facts, it follows that truth cannot be the mind's conformity to reality, even in the case of mundane facts and practical life. For if this concept of language is correct, human knowledge can never be representative, for knowledge as such could not have the nature of a signification of the world. Now, it seems to me that the criticism I have suggested above concerning the semantic interpretation of language is, if anything, truer of everyday, practical language about hard, obstinate facts than of the more rarefied levels and forms of human thought. And it seems to me that the alternative interpretation of language I have suggested in its place is, if anything, truer of, say, scientific than of philosophical and theological thought. For what I have had constantly in mind, both when criticizing the semantic view and when suggesting a syntactic alternative, has been the factuality of the world. Indeed, *the trouble with the traditional concept of truth is that ultimately it would fit only a world in which the facts were more than the facts,* a world in which the facts had an intrinsic meaningfulness and necessity, an *inner truth* which was the ground and cause of the reflected truth of the human mind. Against this supposition stands the view that, for all their hardness, solidity and subborness, the facts are nothing but the facts. What shall we say, then, about the factuality of the facts?

Well, the first thing is precisely that: that the facts have a factual quality. It is indeed this, not their supposed necessity, that makes the facts to be the facts. It is because they are contingent, because they do not have an intrinsic rationality and self-justification, that the facts can be said to be hard and stubborn. Therefore, it is true: the facts are indeed the facts. Who can, by taking thought, add a cubit to his stature, or make white to be black, or change noon to midnight? It is perfectly obvious and undeniable that no one can change the facts by thinking as he may wish. On the other hand, this hardly means that truth is the mind's submission to the inner necessitation of things, to the inward unavoidableness of the structures that make the facts meaningful in themselves. For the facts are known as facts only upon reflection, precisely by distinguishing within our knowledge between ourselves and the truth of human consciousness, on the one hand, and, on the other, the world of reality, the world *in which* the truth of human consciousness structures, I do not say reality, but *man*.

If the facts have to be respected and abided by, the reason is not that they have a right to be respected or a warrant to rule human life. They must be respected and abided by because to contemn them and to abstract from them would be for human consciousness nothing less than presuming to contemn itself and failing to abide by its own nature. In other words, the need to abide by the facts does not reside in the facts, but in consciousness, and it does not mean that truth is extracted from the facts or given by their mental reduplication. When we truthfully say, for instance, that "it is raining outside," then the assertion that "it is raining outside" is not the reflection of a true fact: it is the statement of a truth.[4] This means: the truth is not the fact itself, any more than it is the semantic representation of the fact. It is the quality of consciousness as it abides by the facts. If so, the fact is not the original

---

[4] This is why, as many philosophers have noted, there is no real difference between the judgments "A is B" and "I think that A is B," or "It is true that A is B."

source of truth, whence derives by signification the representative truth of knowledge and speech. The fact is rather what the truth is about.

The implication of this is that the relationship between the facts of reality and the truth of the mind is the opposite of what we are apt to think if we are swayed by the semantic view of language. It is not true that we first know the facts and thereafter acquire the truth about them. On the contrary, it is only on the assumption that our knowledge is true that we can, reflectively and abstractively, point to the facts. To imagine otherwise is to be grossly self-deluded. It is to imagine that we can know something before we can think it. To think that one can know the bare facts before one puts any interpretation on them is to think that one could see the darkness if only one suddenly flashed a powerful searchlight on it.

Thus, the facts are the same for every man, yet the truth is not necessarily the same for all. This is why men disagree on what the facts really are, or on which facts are truly relevant. Indeed, the facts are the same for every creature, but the truth is discovered only by man. The facts drop down from heaven, alike upon the wise and the foolish, the conscious and the brute. Rain makes everyone who stands under it wet. But not every creature that gets wet when it rains is conscious that "it is raining outside," or that this is the assertion of a truth, that is, the true assertion of a fact. This is why it could well be said that man is the only creature on earth who *knows* enough to come in out of the rain. Many beasts take cover against the elements, but they cannot *say* that they are hiding from the weather—and least of all can they dispute among themselves whether the rain does "in fact" stay mainly on the plain. Or, to put it differently, human beings are not protected from the climate by fur or eiderdown but by their cerebral cortex. And they may not be able to do much about changing the weather, but they are able to do what is much more important, namely, to talk about it—for talking about it is the first step towards setting up meteorological services and launching weather satellites, and towards developing a string of Mediterranean resorts along the beautiful Costa Brava of Spain.

In sum, though rain is a universal fact which as such impinges upon all things and upon all life, man is the only animal who knows that raining can be a fact. It is because he can know facts as facts—which he can in turn do, as I have suggested, only because his knowledge can be true or false—that in order to be true his knowledge has to be much more profound and creative than would be the mere accurate and faithful representation of the facts.

In the last analysis, then, the criticism of the semantic interpretation of language implies a criticism of the semantic interpretation of reality. For the semantic view of human consciousness implies a corresponding view of reality as that which is *signifiable* by the mind to itself by means of concepts and judgments, (and by the mind to another by means of words and propositions signifying concepts and judgments). In the philosophical tradition that we have inherited from the Greeks, the ultimate reason why thought can be the signification of reality is that it is the nature of reality to be *signifiable*. That is, in this view there can be meaning (in and for the mind) only because there is a meant (in and for itself). Hence, reality is constituted by its aptitude for being signified or meant: it has, as it were, an inner significance of its own, a meaning in and for itself which makes it to be the very reality it is. There is, then, an inner light to reality, an inner shining truth which is the ground of the reflected truth of human thought and speech. Truth is the conformity of the mind to reality, to begin with, because it is in the nature of the mind to represent reality to itself; but truth is the mind's conformity to reality, ultimately, only because reality has an inner meaningfulness, a necessary structure within itself, which constitutes it precisely as the ground of truth. Thus, in this view language is the outward signification of the mind's inner signification of signifiable reality, to begin with, because it is in the nature of speech to tell what reality is like; but language is the mind's outward signification of the mind's inner signification of signifiable reality, ultimately, only because reality has within itself something which, as it were, calls out for being signified, accosting every mental passer-by with solicitations and requests for being told about.

From the perspective adopted here, however, it would appear more adequate to understand language as self-communication rather than as story-telling. Or perhaps it might be better to say that language is creative of man's selfhood rather than illustrative of the world's objectivity. In either event, the point is that if we try to understand the nature of language without the presupposition that its nature is to be significative, then we are likely to shed at the same time the presupposition that speaking about reality would be idle prattle unless it were speaking about it as it is in-and-for-itself, on the superficially plausible reasoning that if all we know about anything were what it is for us, but not what it is in-and-for-itself, we would not know what it *truly* is.

Does understanding require that there be something which is understood? Yes, of course. But does understanding require that that which is understood be first of all the reality in-and-for-itself of that which is understood, and only derivatively its reality for

86

us? This would be absurd. Rather, it would be superstitious. It would be to suppose that there is an inner, hidden power within every being which holds it together and which draws the mind towards it as a sort of psychomagnetic force. And I have called this idea a superstition deliberately, alluding to its religious source. For this belief in a hidden mind-like principle of reality—the Greeks called it the inner *logos* (word), and the Latins the inner *ratio* (reason)—this faith in a sort of cryptic Medusan spell which reality as such supposedly possesses within its metaphysical recesses, whence it exerts its fatal charm upon the unwary contemplating mind, stands at the earliest point of transition from the primitive Greek religions to the sophisticated, rational religion of Greek philosophy. The very earliest surviving philosophical text of the Hellenic-Western philosophical tradition is, after all, Thales' statement that "all things are full of the gods." The Thalesian divinities have been, of course, thoroughly demythologized in the course of twenty-seven centuries of philosophical development. But the superstitious character of this view does not depend upon the ascription of sacredness, mystery and divinity to the inner reality which all things are supposedly full of. It depends upon the inwardness, the un-apparency (as contrasted with trans-parency) of the reality which supposedly fills all things. The essence of the superstition is the supposition that things are filled with something other than themselves, something which is their real reality; it is the supposition that nothing is really what it seems; that if we are ignorant and un-knowing the reason is not that our skills are undeveloped, but that reality is constituted by a resistant density which defies penetration by the mind.

To this may be contrasted the more empirically oriented supposition that there can be no reality which defines the reality of anything, except the reality itself; and that, therefore, behind the reality of anything, or within it, there is nothing more fundamental and/or real than it itself. Knowledge cannot be the attainment of the inward necessities of things, because things are not filled with necessity. Indeed, they are not filled with anything. They are, as it were, solid through and through: their reality is identical with themselves.

The methodological implications of this view are not the least important of the manifold consequences that flow from it. If the reconsideration of the nature of language along the lines indicated by contemporary research are truly revolutionary, the reason is that its findings provide all human enquiry, regardless of subject matter, with a new perspective. Or, granted that an enquiry is directed towards the ascertainment of some nature, the significance of the modern redefinition of language lies in that it entails a redefinition of the nature of nature.

In the theories of reality devised by the Hellenic-Western philosophical tradition on the basis provided by its assumptions concerning language, the nature of anything was its inner, essential, necessary constitution: the typical behavior and properties of every being were but the consequence of what it was in-and-for-itself. And what it was in-and-for-itself was that inner principle which chartered it and made it definable as the sort of reality it was. The nature of man, for instance, was that intelligible, definable, signifiable reality within him which structured him substantially in himself and which was, therefore, the source of his actions and operations. Now, in what sense was this an *inner* principle? Surely not in the sense that it lay physically, spatially, inside man. It was truly inner, however, in the sense that this nature was his own, proper and distinctive intelligible constitution precisely insofar as he existed in himself, insofar as he was an actually existing being and, thus, insofar as he stood in isolation from every other being in the world. The condition of the possibility of explaining the nature of nature in this manner was, therefore, the assumption of the absoluteness of being as such. To look for the *inner* constitutive principle of anything in order to understand it was to assume that it was intelligible precisely insofar as it was *unrelated* to everything else.

What we are gradually discovering, in the wake of the novel linguistic and philosophical approaches to the study of language such as I have suggested here, and what is even at this early date beginning to overflow into a variety of other disciplines and modes of scientific enquiry and to seep into the collective consciousness of Western culture today, is that, paradoxical though it may seem at first, the intelligible constitution of reality as such is not to be found within things, but rather outside and beyond them. It is to be found, if I may put it less metaphorically, not within things themselves, in their absoluteness, but in their relations to everything else—just as their explanation for us is to be found in their history—and therefore in the processes in which they take part.[5] In the case of man, for instance, this means that human nature is not to be found in the individual substance of man, but in his temporal and historical projections, that is, in the process by which he emerges out of the past towards the future. He who would understand man must, as it were, adopt the motto: *si naturam requires, circumspice.* That is, if you wish to understand the nature of man you must look to the world he brings about, you

[5] This apparently misleads a number of philosophers (the best known of whom is perhaps Whitehead) into thinking that reality as such *is* process. It seems to me better, however, to say that reality as such is relativity—from which it follows, to be sure, that it is *in* process.

must observe how he transforms whatever lies within his horizon, you must examine how he extends and projects himself outwardly in time and space and, above all, you must discover how he gives a distinctive shape to the indeterminate future and thus brings off the creation of history through his consciousness of that which he thinks and believes and does today. And the same is true, in every fundamental respect, of every other reality. It is true even of the reality of God. Or it is not true, as the ancient Christian tradition has it, that if man would know God he should look to that which God has created and made relative to himself by relating himself to it?

To sum up, the criticism of the semantic concept of language leads to an alternative philosophical orientation which might perhaps be best defined by the following points. Language is a functional-syntactic system which gives thought a concrete socio-cultural communicative form. Consciousness is linguistic self-relation to reality. And reality is relativity, diffusiveness and communicativeness: its property is transcendence, that is, leading beyond itself. Truth is the transcendence that is typical of man.

Evidently, this sort of philosophical orientation could not but imply profound consequences for all issues pertaining to religious belief. A few illustrations of these will now be considered, in the second part of this book.

PART II

ISSUES AND ILLUSTRATIONS

4.

Faith and Experience

In the last two chapters I have contrasted the idea that language is semantic in nature (that is, *significative of* experience and, therefore, of reality) with the idea that language is essentially syntactic (that is, *functional in* the com-position of experience and, therefore, in man's self-relation to reality). The former is the essence of the most common interpretations of language since Aristotle to Bertrand Russell: language is a system of signs, that is, pointers, tokens, labels or other counterparts of reality, mediated by thought. This view is often, though not always, further developed into the doctrine that concepts (or "mental words") are signified directly by (spoken) words, whereas concepts are, in turn, the signs which signify reality and thus make reality known. In any event, the philosophy involved in this type of theory of language presupposes, among others, two views. First: that there is a meaningful structure, a signifiable content, or an inner intelligible constitution within reality, which is the object of human understanding and of subsequent human speech. That is, reality is the original, of which language is a counterpart. But this meaningful structure is so complicated, this signifiable content is so variegated, this intelligible structure is so rich, that it must be signified (that is, its meaning must be extracted and subsequently expressed) by means of a multiplicity of different signs. Thus it is that many different things may be said of one and the same thing. But in every case what is signified is, as the common expressions put it, "the truth of the matter," or "what actually is the case," or "the real state of affairs," namely, a fact or complex of facts which contains in itself, and without reference to consciousness, that which in-and-for-itself constitutes the *signifiable* reality which, through knowledge, becomes *signified* by the mind.

The semantic concept of language presupposes, second, that this intelligible content, being a constituent of the reality of being as such, and being *had* by reality in-and-for-itself, is essentially separate from cognition (and, therefore, all the more so from language, since language signifies reality only by first signifying thought). Likewise, the inner meaning of any reality is unrelated to the reality of every other being (and, therefore, all the more so to the reality of the mind that may know it, since the mind has to signify it to itself before it knows that reality). Thus, according to these philosophies cognition and thought (and, therefore, also the outward, linguistic expression of cognition and thought), essentially consist in relating realities which are originally unrelated. The cognitional and cogitative relation which is established by the initiative, vitality and creativity of the knower is *reduplicative* or *presentative* of reality. (Of course, the nature of this reduplication, this re-enactment by the mind of the perfection of the known, and this presentation, this *rendez-vous* with reality, is variously to be understood according to various thinkers.) But these two views taken together mean, in short, that language and thought (on the side of the subject) are distinct and separate from the reality which (on the side of the object) they reduplicate. Linguistic signification is but the exteriorization or *ex-pression* of cognitive reduplication. Speech is essentially representative and reduplicative of reality, albeit through the mediation of thought. Language is supposed to *tell* what reality is like.

It follows, of course, that language (like the thought behind language) must conform to reality—or else it will be, if not mere babbling and raving, at least an inadequate or misleading account of reality, that is, a telling that does not really tell what reality is like. The linguistic reduplication of reality must, albeit analogously, *parallel* reality; otherwise it would, by definition, diverge from reality. If so, it would be deceptive, whether because it did not truly express what one did know (in which case one would be lying), or because it did (in which case one was mistaken). Thus, the conformity theory of truth is essentially a *semantic* theory of truth. Language tells outwardly what cognition and thought tell inwardly, namely, what reality is, or what it is like. If so, it is obvious that, if I may so put it, either language and thought tell it like it is, or they do not. If they do, they are right; otherwise they are wrong. To understand correctly is "to grasp the truth" and, therefore, to be in a position to express it in words, that is, "to tell the truth of the matter."

As an alternative to the foregoing, a functional, syntactic interpretation of language would conceive language as the means whereby man can situate himself in the world and create his selfhood out of his relation to reality. Language is expressive and creative of the human self. The philosophical consequences of this view are accordingly at variance with those which we have just seen. Though we may well wish—why not?—to retain such expression as "telling the truth of the matter" (and indeed such expressions as "expression," despite the fact that in this view "expression" is not the mind's utterance of what it had previously extracted from reality), to tell the truth or to grasp the true state of affairs is not to reduplicate the inner meaning of reality by means of spoken words or, in the first place, by means of "mental words" (concepts, judgments and syllogisms). This is to be rejected not only because neither language nor thought are of a significative nature, but also because they do not stand opposite a reduplicatable, signifiable reality or intelligible, meaningful, constitutive structure of a reality which is in itself, and precisely as real, unrelated to every other reality. At least, this is what would follow once it were agreed that language is the *matrix* of thought, not its *expression,* and that cognition is the self-creative activity of conscious selfhood as it differentiates and opposes itself to the world of objects from which it is originally indistinct.

Language, therefore, does not duplicate reality. It is the formal means whereby consciousness thinks about reality, that is, empirically relates itself to it. Language is not the token of reality. It is not a label for, or a pointer to, the meaning which exists in reality. It is the embodiment and concretization—that is, it is the symbolization—of the meaning created by man's self-relation to a strictly factual and absolutely contingent reality. Thus, language does not *tell* what reality is like, or what we think it is like. Rather, it crystallizes our knowledge of reality, that is, our conscious, purposive self-relation to it. Language is the concrete actualization at a given moment of our self-creativity *in relation to* some determinate object out of the vast reality of being in the world. Language forms and makes possible man's self-relation to reality.

From this it follows, far from the usual opinion that the prior conformity of my thought to reality enables me to make statements which correspond to reality, that my statements are true if they render my thinking true, and that it is having a true linguistic form that makes my thinking to be true, not the other way about. But what makes any given linguistic form to be true?

If what I have suggested so far is correct, the epistemic value, the truth-value, of language [1] does not hinge, therefore, on whether language depicts or represents reality faithfully (since it does not depict or represent reality at all, in the first place), but on whether it performs its essential function well. That is, the truth-value of language hinges on its relative adequacy or effectiveness in the formation of consciousness. Hence, my language is false (and not merely mendacious) if it deceives *me*—rather, if I deceive myself when I think what I say. As for this self-deception, it occurs when I elaborate my consciousness so as to construe the world (that is, to establish my meaningful relations to it) in a manner which, granted the actual world situation in which I am and become consciously human, does not in point of historical fact contribute to my being and my becoming consciously human.

If I think that arsenic is a harmless condiment, I, not arsenic, am much the worse off for it. And this is not merely because I am likely to make a mess of the stew, but also because by so thinking I have formed myself in a way which places me at a disadvantage for further thinking about the world. Sooner or later, if my error is important enough, I will have, as it were, to go back and set *myself* aright—the world was never touched by my mistake. I have to undo, and then re-do, my biography, in however small and inconsequential part. For I exist in a world in which arsenic in fact is (as those of us who *already* know this are entitled to say) truly poisonous, not a harmless condiment. When I thought otherwise my error did not consist in my crossing up

[1] In contrast to other possible values, like usefulness—but values which are, however, closely related to and dependent upon the primary linguistic value, which is truth.

reality or contradicting it—after all, *it* does not really say anything, does it?—or in my failure to signify it to myself as it really was. My error was pure and simply my failure to exist and to make myself be in the only world that actually exists. It was, thus, my failure to create myself in this particular, ordinarily inconsequential, way, and my creating instead only a partly unviable self, a partly unreal self, out of my self-relation to the world.

I trust I have made the point clear. To say that the epistemic value of statements is not given by their conformity to reality does *not* mean that I can, with truth, say whatever I wish, regardless of what reality may be. I repeat: the situation in which I am conscious, and in which I must consciously determine myself, and in which I must think, is given, and it is antecendent to my consciousness of it. Hence, it is perfectly true, though this truth is the object of much misinterpretation, that true statements *do,* in point of fact, more or less approximately conform to reality. This really means: true statements embody man's greater or lesser adequacy to the real situation in which he exists and is conscious (or, in my terminology, language is *symbolic,* not *significative*). It does not mean, however, that truth consists in such adequacy, or least of all in the statement's conformity to reality. Statements are adequate, and even conform to reality, *because* they are true. What I would deny is that statements are true because they (or the thoughts "behind" them) enjoy the condition of adequation to reality, or because they conform to it.

Now, I suggested at the outset of this book that there are clear and direct connections between the changes in man's self-understanding and the contemporary Catholic crisis, because philosophical ideas have a clear and direct connection with religious thought. This is perhaps most obviously true—and not least important—in what pertains to the religious idea of faith, since all concrete religious beliefs are decisively shaped by the underlying conscious or unconscious, tacit or explicit, assumptions of the believer concerning the nature of belief.

I need scarcely recall in much detail the standard Catholic theology of faith in order to show how faithfully it assumes all the philosophical positions which stem from the semantic view of language, which I have criticized above. It begins with the perfectly self-evident proposition that God, the object of belief, does not lend itself to immediate experience. But it continues with the assumption that human experience is some sort of inward reception of a cognitive content or truth. Religious consciousness is thus some sort of inward reception of an objective, divine truth. To attempt to explain the nature of faith is to attempt to explain how the human mind can receive a truth without seeing it, how it can possess truth without evidence, how it can assert anything about God without having seen him. Thus, the very position of the theological problem of the nature of faith assumes that faith is a sort of imperfect knowledge, a lesser form of knowledge which substitutes for real knowledge. Of course, this theology will also emphasize that this lesser sort of knowledge is nevertheless superior to all other knowledge available to man in this world, because its status as a lesser sort of knowledge is offset by the nobility and certainty of the truths that this imperfect mode of knowledge puts us in possession of. But faith is nevertheless an essentially imperfect mode of knowledge, since it is the assent of the intellect to truths it does not see. The intellect does this because, when the absence of evidence leaves it undetermined and uncertain, the will commands it to determine itself by assenting to inevident truths. However, this does not make the act of faith

99

arbitrary or irrational. It is not arbitrary, because the will is, in the first instance, moved by divine grace. And it is not irrational, because the truths proposed for our assent rest upon the infallible authority of God, who is neither deceptive nor deceived.

I will not deal here with all the difficulties that have historically emerged in the history of Christianity with this idea of faith. I will but mention one which is particularly important in our times, and which is directly relevant to my thesis. If faith is assent to a truth revealed by God, an assent given on the basis of God's authority rather than on the basis of our vision of the truth, then the formulation or conceptualization of the truths of human faith lies outside the realm of human experience. In this view, the truth of faith is literally a divine truth, for it is the truth of God's own understanding of himself; it is the truth of God himself transplanted into a human mind which can but mindlessly hold it, nodding to itself that, whatever it may mean, it holds within itself a divinely guaranteed truth.

The absurdity of this interpretation of the nature of faith is not evident as long as man remains sufficiently unaware of the nature of human consciousness to fail to realize that, as Edward Schillebeeckx has put it, "the world of human experience is the only access to the saving reality of revelation and faith. For that matter, how could be listen to a revelation from God—how can it be a revelation to man, if it falls outside our experience? It is impossible for man to know or to be aware of realities which man does not experience in one way or another." [2] Or, to put it epigrammatically, the traditional idea of faith supposes that Hebrew and Greek are God's mother tongues. More precisely, no concept of

[2] "Faith functioning in human self-understanding," in T. Patrick Burke, *The Word in History,* (New York, 1966), p. 45.

faith can be reasonably advanced today unless it attempts to understand how faith functions in human experience; no analysis of faith can be sound unless it be an analysis of faith as a form of human experience.

Such an analysis need not take away from the traditional conviction that faith is in a very real sense given by grace. For such an analysis might well indicate that the essential and primary function of faith is to embody man's reaction to a situation which is not of his own doing. Faith originates when man suddenly discovers himself to be *already* existing, and to be part of an ongoing world which is already in process. This may or may not justify the conclusion that Someone created the world, and that man had better pay attention to such a powerful agent. But it does imply a commitment to conceive oneself and to guide oneself according to the view that the initiative which brings ourselves and the world of being into being does not lie within ourselves.

Faith is not, therefore, merely man's understanding of himself. On the other hand, neither is it a guessing at God, or a divination of arcane truths, or a blind probing into the cosmic fog. Faith is man's self-understanding, but precisely as relative to a transcendent reality beyond his own, and man's self-disposition in the presence of a transcendent reality beyond himself. Faith, is, therefore, on the one hand, the manifestation of man to himself, in the sense that man's consciousness of existence defines him to himself as an essentially religious animal. On the other hand, when consciousness manifests man to himself, it manifests him as a reality who in his very being, and even in his consciousness of being, is relative to a reality which is not measured by man's being, or even by man's consciousness of being. It matters little whether we call this reality God, and even less whether we give it a proper name at all—though in this connection I am reminded of the wisdom of the Rumanian writer Petru Dumitriu: if we call God "Father," why not also "Uncle," and if we address him as "Lord," might we not as well say "Dear Sir," or "Dear Comrade"?[3]

In any event, in the view I have been suggesting, faith is, far from a foreign element in human experience, an integral part of it. Faith is that aspect or dimension or modality of consciousness that gives to human experience its basic meaningfulness. Belief in God is scarcely some sort of apprehension of an eternal truth. On the other hand, if our belief in God does not enhance the meaningfulness of the world in which we actually and presently exist by referring that world beyond itself, then Christian belief in God would be difficult to distinguish from primitive magic, except perhaps in degree of irresponsibility. By which I mean that, whereas primitive cultures have steadily contributed to the development of human consciousness through the elaboration of primitive religions, Christianity could not be credited with unique validity and with singular truth if in the end it were to function as but a primitive religion writ large, a primitive religion which happened to be the true one because its God happened to be the real God.

But what I should in conclusion stress is that the conception of faith to which I have been alluding differs from the traditional view not nearly so much in the conclusions that follow from it as in the premises which lead to it—I mean, premises concerning human experience, human nature and human phenomena. For instance, one of the premises that renders possible the traditional Catholic theology of faith is that assent to inevident truths does

[3] See J. A. T. Robinson, *Exploration into God,* (Stanford, 1967), p. 93.

not make faith irrational or uncertain in the case of the truths of revelation, because these truths have been revealed by the God who, being Truth itself, can hardly deceive or be deceived. Now, the Catholic tradition has never been so naïve as to be totally unaware of the possible objection to the foregoing reasoning: surely, it might be said, it is not evident that these truths have been revealed by God and that they must be assented to because of their divine authority; surely faith's assent to these truths presupposes the prior belief that they have been truly revealed. And on what authority is to be believed the proposition that these truths have been revealed, which did not itself require a prior act of faith in order to be taken precisely as an authority?

The traditional Catholic answer to this objection is simple: the revelation of God is not a private affair. It would not be reasonable to expect God to instruct each and every individual in the divine truths. But even if it were, this is not in any event the way in which God has in fact chosen to reveal himself. Revelation takes place above all in the institution of a doctrinal tradition and in the establishment of a competent teaching office which perpetuates and preserves the deposit of faith. In short, belief in the truths authoritatively revealed by God begins with belief in the teaching authority of the Church. For the Christian, belief in God is inseparable from belief in God's Church. In a very real sense, therefore, to believe in the Church is to believe in God, just as to believe in God is to believe in the Church.

I hope I will not confuse you if I confess that I find this reasoning fundamentally true and convincing. Although the Reformation—correctly, as I believe—took issue with the identification of the authoritative magisterium with the hierarchy and the papacy, in my opinion it nevertheless failed to retain a sufficient sense of the social and historical nature of the process of revelation. The exaltation of Scripture and of private judgment may have been intended to correct the divinization of tradition and of hierarchical and papal judgment, but I am not persuaded that it was a sufficiently adequate solution. In any event, I think it is in principle reasonable to propose that individuals place their act of religious faith only through social and historical processes—for instance, through the tradition of the Christian community. What may not be reasonable is to suppose that this act of faith is but the precondition to assenting to divinely revealed truths, because this would in effect make faith in God the equivalent of the abdication of one's conscience in favour of someone else's. The truth of revelation is not a truth that stands hidden behind the social and historical processes which are the Church. The truth of revelation is the truth of those very processes; it is the truth manifested in the social and historical reality of the Church. On the other hand, I ask you to consider that during epochs when all human relations have been predicated on the principle that order is necessarily pyramidical, the traditional theology of faith was not far out of line with ordinary human experience. If superiority-inferiority ruled all interpersonal relationships and, of course, above all the relation of creator and creature, God and man, did it not make sense to think that the revelation of God, which is carried in a socio-historical tradition, should depend upon the authoritative teaching of the Church, understood as the superior wisdom and the commanding spiritual power of the Church?

I need not remind you that this is the way in which many authorities in the Catholic Church still reason today. The teaching authority, they think, has been entrusted by God with certain truths about himself. Though no one should be forced to assent to the truths taught by such authority, even if they are truths whose ultimate authority derives from God, faith can only be understood as assent to such truths, precisely as taught by the teaching authority of the Church. Anyone who thinks otherwise may well please himself—at the cost of his eternal salvation, to be sure—but is hardly entitled to call himself a Catholic, in the traditional sense of this term.

This brings us to the topic of my next chapter. Meanwhile, I will but remark once again that even such brief discussion as I have had time for in the latter part of this lecture should begin to illustrate my contention: conflicts of opinion on the most abstruse theological issues in the Catholic Church today ultimately resolve in conflicts of opinion about matters of fundamental attitudes towards human experience and everyday life. The traditional theology of faith and its objections to the concept of belief as a form of experience depend not merely upon the wish to respect the traditional Christian faith, but also upon the wish to retain the traditional cultural form of that faith. My suggestion, which I plan to elaborate in the next two chapters, is that we may well share the first wish without having to share the second, and that the resolve to reject the second may well be the best means to fulfill the first.

5.

Church and Authority

I have maintained here that the Catholic crisis is in a very real sense not so much a division of the Church on matters of faith as on matters of human reason and judgment, matters that have to do with human experience, and matters which are the proper object of philosophical thought. We think we are divided on the loftiest and most abstract issues. In a way, this is true. But we are divided on these only because we are first split by different mentalities, different customs, different modes of experiencing the reality of the world and the reality of man in everyday life. On the other hand, although our divisions may not originally pertain to matters of faith, faith is ultimately affected very deeply just the same. As we have just seen, the very idea of faith itself is a function of some prior idea of human consciousness. Contemporary Catholic traditionalism finds it impossible to countenance any view of faith that did not somehow reduce faith to assent on the basis of authority. This would be, ultimately, God's own authority. But since God does not authoritatively reveal himself privately, but only socially and historically, the authority on which the assent of faith must be based is, mediately, the authority of the magisterium of the Church. Hence, the great preoccupation of so many in the Catholic Church, and in the first place Pope Paul, with the problem of authority.

Now, it would seem at first that this problem, if no other, is self-contained and definable without reference to epistemological questions. For it may appear simply a question whether submission to the magisterium in matters of morals and doctrine is or is not demanded of the Catholic believer by virtue of his faith. On the assumption that this is truly the problem some would argue, as the Pope has done, that an examination of Scripture and tradition yields an unqualified affirmative answer, whereas others would argue that such an examination yields a much more sophisticated idea of authority, and that a qualified negative answer to this question does not take away any papal or magisterial authority as such, but only its abuse.

I would not want to belittle in the slightest the importance of the work of those scholars who have attacked the problem in the latter way. On the other hand, the proper reply to the proposition that God demands submissiveness to the teaching of his appointed representatives is *not* that religious truth has to do only, or primarily, with individual conscience, and nothing, or little, or only secondarily, to do with authority. Yet, not a few debates in recent times have been predicated on just such premises. The conflict is, of course, irresoluble as long as it is fought on these grounds, for the very good reason that, in one way, both sides are right, but that, in another, both are wrong.

If one looks at the matter impartially, one can well understand the Pope's consternation as he finds that his teaching authority is not merely questioned but even widely rejected. For the Pope is undoubtedly right when he recalls that in the uninterrupted tradition of many centuries the necessary correlate of the Catholic faith has always been a minimal degree of submissiveness and docility to the teaching office of the Pope, on the ground that such office derived its authority from divine institution.[1] On the other hand, an impartial look at the problem should also find it very easy to understand the feeling of those who, in all intellectual honesty, conclude that the Pope could not very well expect anyone to take him seriously, least of all authoritatively, when his teaching in so many respects appears to lack not only wisdom, but even elementary common sense. Perhaps such dissenters should be told that to arrogate to oneself the faculty of judging the common sense of the papal teaching would be precisely to set oneself up as a higher authority than the magisterium, and that this would depart from the traditional Catholic understanding of the implications of belief.

But this argument against the dissenters will simply not do. It is true that human reason is fallible; therefore, anyone would be imprudent to think that he can be certain of the boundary between the possible and the impossible, between what he understands and what may well be true. On the other hand, it is far from presumptuous for anyone, even for him who recognizes his own fallibility and inadequacy, to judge, as he willy-nilly must, about the good sense of any position to which he might have to commit his existence and character. In other words, there is a natural and unavoidable limit to the ability of man to suspend judgment or to abdicate his conscience. For the disclaimer to competence or to wisdom, or the decision to abdicate one's conscience in favour of someone else's, requires a judgment to that very effect. If I say, for instance, "Perhaps you know better than I, and therefore I will defer to your judgment," I have implicitly judged that it makes sense to recognize the possibility that perhaps you *do*

[1] With, moreover, "divine institution" understood in a fairly fundamentalist sense. Cf. below, note 2.

know better than I. What no one can do is sincerely to say "Perhaps you know better than I" at the same time that he thinks that you are not making much sense, or that you are altogether missing the point.

But I seem to have overbalanced my argument now towards the side of private judgment. Perhaps I should return once again to the other opinion and recall that, in point of fact, countless Catholic believers in the past have found it perfectly possible to listen to much the same papal teachings as those which now cause dissent, without feeling that common sense had been outraged. They have, in effect, judged, "Perhaps the Church knows better than I, even if its teaching makes no sense to me, because evidently, this only means that I am not qualified to tell what is and what is not sound common sense." Catholics appear to have long felt that no consideration of good sense could militate against their taking the teaching of the magisterium of the Church as an unquestionable truth ultimately guaranteed by the veracity of the revealing God. Why, then, can so many Catholics not do likewise today? That is the question that the Pope and other Church authorities have put to themselves in public in recent times, either finding no answer, or else concluding that the answer points to someone's moral fault—and if not to any man's, then to the evil of the nether powers that are loose in the world.

It seems to me, however, that if we consider the changing nature of teaching, the evidence points to an altogether different sort of answer. In the tradition of many centuries of Christian culture, teaching in general has been conceived as the imparting or communication of truth. The teacher knew some truth or possessed a certain intellectual virtue: this truth and this virtue were subsequently exteriorized and concretized in language and other signs, so that the learner could, through the mediation of these signs, posit within himself the truth which proceeded from the teacher. In this manner, through the instrumentality of the teacher, the learner could acquire within himself the same intellectual virtue that characterized the teacher's knowledge. Correspondingly, the teacher's authority, his moral title to teach and to draw upon the student's docility, accrued to him on account of his possession of knowledge and truth. The teacher as such had a right to expect being heeded: teaching was essentially authoritative, and as such it called for respect and submissiveness on the part of him who was taught.

Now, these were the characteristics of all teaching. The teaching authority of the Church was not different in nature from the teaching authority of any other teacher. Of course, the Church had infinitely greater teaching authority than any other teacher, because the source of its truth was the infinite Truth itself. For the truth taught by the magisterium of the Church was not, of course, the truth of the human beings who happened to occupy the teaching office, but the truth of the revelation of God as given in deposit to the Church.[2] Thus, the degree, and the magnitude,

[2] Much of the difficulty in this connection is caused not only by the factors which we will study in the remainder of this chapter, but also by another one, which must be at least briefly considered, namely, the fundamentalist or quasi-fundamentalist conception of revelation that still prevails at most levels of the Catholic Church. The essential feature of it is the idea that revelation is, I do not say man's acquisition of a religious truth to which his own nature could not lay claim as his due, but man's acquisition of someone else's truth, namely, God's, about himself. Hence, in the Christian theological tradition, which presupposes the self-delimited, self-enclosed, self-sufficient and self-necessitated character of human nature, as well as the unitive and reduplicative character of human experience, a distinction has been frequently made between "natural religion," which is praiseworthy but insufficient unto its very ends, and "revealed religion," which

and the warrant of its teaching authority may have been peculiar to the Church, but its teaching was authoritative in the first place only because it was in the nature of all teaching to be so. That is, all teaching derived its authority from the possession of truth.

If the teaching authority of the Church is compromised today, the reason is not necessarily that people nowadays have little interest in the truth, or that they are unwilling to be taught, or that

is alone sufficiently valid and true. The difference between the two is precisely that natural religion is that knowledge of God which man can obtain through the exercise of his natural powers, whereas revealed religion, as the name implies, is God's communication to man of God's own wisdom and truth about himself—so that, presumably, man's nature and human experience have essentially nothing to do with it.

At first sight this distinction seems water-tight—at least in the sense that it would seem perfectly possible in itself. When we reflect upon it, however, certain difficulties begin to appear. In the first place, the distinction itself is of human origin, insofar as it is the result of an apologetic, speculative effort to explain the uniqueness of the Judaeo-Christian tradition in view of the later belief of that very tradition in the universality of mankind's creaturely relationship to God—which implies that the uniqueness of this tradition must be somehow related to the variety of human religious traditions. It could not be easily claimed, therefore, that the distinction is itself revealed. And this would in turn imply the paradox that the work of human reason can sustain the validity of revelation, (cf. above, Chapter 1). We need not pursue this difficulty, but I have deemed it worth mentioning because it may serve as a symbol of the difficulties of apologetic theology, which not infrequently suffers from an excess of zeal. On the other hand, I wish to make it clear that the apologetic and speculative origin of the distinction between natural and revealed religion does not necessarily invalidate the beliefs and the religious truths that it attempts to support. But it is fair warning that the question of the nature of religion in general, and of Judaeo-Christianity in particular, is not as simple as Christian theologians may have thought in the past. The point I am trying to make, therefore, is not that there cannot be any "revealed" religion in any meaningful sense of the term, but that "revelation" should not be literally, fundamentalistically understood. It may well be that the ultimate origin and validity of "revealed" religion involves more than man. In any event, revealed religion may not be fittingly or properly opposed to natural religion. Conversely, there may be a truly "revelatory" quality to the so-called they resist listening to anything but that which suits them. On the contrary, the difficulty may in part be, not that many Catholics have itchy ears, but that they may have eager minds. For it appears that the human mind has developed, and one of the consequences of its development has been a rising standard of expectation in understanding. However, they are correct who suspect that this change in mentality is a novelty in the history of the natural religions which lie outside the Judaeo-Christian tradition.

But we should leave this aside, since more important is, second, the consideration that the concept of revealed religion, in the specific sense which is implied by its opposition to natural religion, is at bottom a contradiction in terms. For, as we have just seen, revealed religion is distinguished from natural religion largely by the ascription of its wisdom to a supra-human source rather than to human nature. The difficulty with this is that it presupposes the mutual *exclusiveness* of human nature and such supra-mundane source, at the same time that it presupposes *communication* from this transcendent source to man. Now, if communication to man were possible (as the traditional semantic theories of language ordinarily allow) in the absence of all human experience of what is communicated, this might not imply a contradiction. But communication to human consciousness requires the exercise of human consciousness, and the communication of God's own wisdom to man would require not only the passive, but the active, self-present exercise of man's conscious nature. However "divine," therefore, the wisdom and the truth of revelation must in some basic sense also be man's. For example, the categories, the concepts, the ideas of revealed religion must be human categories, human concepts and human ideas, if they are going to be effectively communicative at all. It is well and good to say that the wisdom and the truth of religious belief do not derive their ultimate authority and validity from man. It is quite another thing, however, to imagine that this wisdom and this truth are therefore in no sense natural—or that their human, natural form negates their transcendental value. In other words, the notion that revelation is a *communication* (to man) implies that human nature, and specifically human consciousness and experience, are essentially involved in it. For any language that man can understand is, by that very fact, human in form. Therefore, to say that there are "revealed" truths is to say that these truths enter into human experience. And to say that they enter human experience is to say that they must be in some sense natural to man. The language of revelation is human, even if the truth of it reaches beyond man. Revelation is, therefore, in a very real sense natural to man.

113

Church. For the intellectual eagerness of Catholics in recent times has not been developed from inner resources within the Church: it has been largely learned from the non-Catholic and in particular from the secular world. Thus, to the extent that many Church authorities and officials have isolated themselves from the human reality of the developing secular world, and most particularly from the intellectual world—or to the degree that they have been willy-

---

Once again we reach the conclusion, not that the concept of revelation is necessarily invalid, but that it must be recast in order to make allowance for man's greater awareness of his own nature—and in particular of his greater awareness of the self-present character of human consciousness. Conversely, as long as Church authorities are burdened by the misapprehension that the "deposit of faith" is a set of linguistic signs which enshrine God's own self-understanding and which must, therefore, be preserved intact under pain of betrayal, the teaching authority will be shackled by its felt duty to be above all the custodian of the past, and not the architect of the future.

Moreover, if we reflect upon the traditional concept of revealed religion, we may observe that it actually implies a certain concept of human nature, and that it assumes a certain human self-understanding. It assumes, if you will, certain views about the nature of language, the nature of communication, and the passivity of human consciousness. It is indeed because of a development in man's self-understanding that the traditional Christian belief in the uniquely transcendent, supra-human character of Christianity, which at one time was fittingly conceptualized in the distinction between natural and revealed religion, must now be conceptualized in another way. Therefore, the suggestion that religion has essentially to do not with God's but with man's self-understanding is not so far removed from the traditional view as might appear at first sight. That traditional view did indeed assume a certain human self-understanding. But it was unaware of this assumption and, therefore, it confused the transcendental, trans-human validity of religious belief with the supposedly extra-human character of revelation and religion. Conversely, it may well be that a certain faith, like Christianity, is truly valid, that it may be truly said to respond to the self-"revelation" of a transcendent reality or God. This does not necessarily take away, however, the human situation, the natural location, as it were, in which that transcendental "revelation" takes place. (Cf. my *Foundations of Belief*, pp. 466–471.)

114

nilly isolated from it by the very nature of their situation—a split has naturally sundered the hierarchy from the growing number of those members of the Church whose consciousness has been affected by the cultural evolution of man, a split that, unfortunately, has become noticeable only after it has reached abysmal depth. In any event, the level of educational attainment of Catholics, particularly in what concerns the *methods* of modern scholarship, has risen sharply all over the Western world in the twentieth century. Well, it was in the course of raising their educational norms that large numbers of Catholics rose to that level of human self-understanding at which the crisis of authority in the Church takes place today.

For one of the most significant events in the history of the relations of Church and world in recent times is that many Catholics have now begun fully to participate in the intellectual and other evolutionary forms of human biological growth without thereby finding it necessary to renounce their faith. Many Catholics have thus *learned to learn* as it has become possible to learn in modern times. The trouble is that the magisterium has *not learned to teach* in a correspondingly advanced way. For people today typically learn—or at least *can* learn—in a different way than they once did. That is why no teacher today—at least, not in any reasonably up-to-date educational environment—understands his task to be that of conveying the truth, or even that of handing on information, but rather, as the jargon goes, that of facilitating the creation of a learning situation. Teaching is not a Socratic task of intellectual midwifery, as if the truth had been fully formed somewhere, merely waiting to be born or to be created in some mind. Nor should the teacher imagine that he moulds the tender mind or shapes the malleable materials of the uninformed intellect. The teacher renders a personal service: and teaching, at least ideally, is an interpersonal relation. This does not mean that teaching is necessarily an affective relationship: it need not be even a highly personalized personal relationship. But it is an essentially interpersonal activity, in the sense that it does not consist in the transmission of truth, or even facilitating the independent discovery of truth by another, but in the creation of an environment in which a mind, a person and a character can create themselves. The teacher today, at least ideally and normatively, does not seek to produce learning, but enquiry; he does not attempt to facilitate the emergence of truth and comprehension, but of truthfulness and creativity.

Hence, the learning role of which most people in our culture are capable today, and to which most people have become more or less consciously accustomed, is not that of accepting the truth, but that of taking an active role in its pursuit and experimental discovery. Truth is a means to the creation of the self. Truth, however speculative and theoretical, has above all a personal dimension. Many people today, even Catholics, suspect this, even if they cannot always conceptualize it to themselves in these terms. But it could therefore be truly said that, in a very real sense, man's capacity for truth has increased. This is, of course, no cause for self-congratulation: it only means that nowadays man must participate more consciously and deliberately in his own self-fashioning than it has been necessary or possible in the past. And the other side of this biological fact is that man's capacity for error, and for evil, is correspondingly greater too. And it matters little whether the statistical increase in the prevalence of this capacity— and of its correlative expectations—does modern man credit, (though it is hardly to his shame and it is undoubtedly to his

116

advantage). For it is in any event a fact. What matters is that man's increased capacity for self-creativity implies a profound shift in the relationship between educator and educand.

For this means that today's teacher gains his prestige by, and his warrant for teaching becomes acceptable because of, and his usefulness and effectiveness as a teacher formally depends upon, not his possession of the truth, but whatever *leadership* he may exercise. Thus, in the Church today, as outside the Church, no teacher can expect to be listened to simply because he "has" the truth, and he cannot expect actually to teach anyone simply by telling him the truth. Indeed, in the extreme case, some of today's best teachers do not themselves know as much truth as they manage to bring out in others. The charismatic teacher can generate more wisdom—for that matter, he can generate more evil—than he has within himself. In this connection mention might be made of John XXIII, one of the most powerful shapers of the contemporary Catholic mind. It is curious to note that most Catholics think of him as a liberal, whereas they think of Pope Paul as a conservative, when in reality, as a comparative analysis of their actual doctrine should reveal, John XXIII's teaching was on the whole much less progressive than that of Pope Paul. If Pope Paul's teaching is not more effective than it actually is—and in some respects, for instance, in the ethics of international relations, this is nothing short of tragic—the reason is not that he has nothing new, or useful, or even progressive to teach, but that his idea of what teaching is is much less adequate than one could hope.

This is, of course, understandable. Pope Paul's problem is, in a way, not unlike that of many parents today, who were themselves formed by a style of parental teaching which even a generation ago or two was already falling behind the evolutionary reality of

117

human nature, but which is drastically inadequate today. It is difficult for many parents today—and I know this from personal experience—to bring up children who, for example, have grown up with television, cramming into eight years the experience which their parents took twenty to accumulate. Ironically, a parent's own experience of having been well brought up can sometimes become a liability today. Well, I will not pretend that I know how best to bring up children, but I think I know what the worst way to do so is, namely, by default to abdicate parental responsibility. However, I am fairly certain that I know what the most useless is, namely, to invoke parental authority and superior experience. It is true that not infrequently Father knows best. The trouble is that Father's knowledge is often irrelevant, and sometimes even countervailing.

This is why, generally speaking, all teaching authority carries a much more onerous burden of responsibility today than at any previous time. If teaching authority today is to be discharged responsibly, not to say also effectively, it must rest, not upon the commanding power of truth, but upon imagination, creativity, experimental sense and the ability to personalize relationships. In a word, teaching authority today is authoritative only insofar as it offers genuine leadership. The teaching authority of the Church today can be neither authoritative nor actually educational unless it consists above all in the exercise of leadership.

And yet, it could not be said that the contemporary Catholic Church suffers from a surfeit of leadership among those in positions of authority. To be sure, leadership is not altogether lacking. There is the select roster of certain well-known European bishops. But their list is not very long. And, of course, there are other bishops elsewhere. Their list is even shorter. Perhaps it is only fair also to say that many bishops are not in a position to exercise much leadership. That may well be. Whatever the reason, the fact is that a good deal of the authoritative teaching of the Church today shows insufficient leadership. If this is correct, the great problem of authority in the Church today is not so much, as some think, that the teaching authority is flouted, or, as others claim, that it is non-existent, or illegitimate or abused. The problem may well be that the teaching authority of the Church is not sufficiently effective because, though it is frequently much too authoritarian, it does not usually assume enough authority for itself. Conversely, the greater danger to the Church may be posed, not so much by those who flout authority because they lack discipline or good sense, as by those who press Church authorities to ply them with infallible certitudes and to confirm them in their backwardness, their ignorance and their intellectual sloth. Indeed, if hierarchical authority is flouted, and if the teaching authority of the Pope in particular is not always respected, part of the reason may be that the Pope and the hierarchy do not always make use of the full authoritative warrant that they *do* have.

For the Church does indeed have authority, and its government has executive power. This means: its task is not mindlessly to relay messages from heaven, or to carry out divine orders according to standing regulations and by the book, or to perform errands for God. The government of the Church must use its initiative and creativity in order to discharge its trust. The Church has been given doctrinal talents not to keep safe but to invest. This is the sense in which I have elsewhere suggested that the Church has a mission, not a message. The mission, to be sure, involves teaching and doctrine and truth. But the Church is the living Body of Christ, and Christ was not a messenger from God, but his self-revelation. Likewise, the Church does not convey a message from God, but manifests him in his real presence among men. In other words, the Church has no message from God, because the Church *is* a message from God. For the Church proclaims or, rather, manifests the living reality of God not simply in its external language and other signs but in its inner living reality. The problem, in short, may be that the teaching authority of the Church needs reconceptualization in order to have any real relation to the human situation that in fact exists today.

It may well be objected that this proposal leaves out of account the crucial point, namely, that regardless of all consideration of pedagogical efficiency, the magisterium must retain its traditional understanding of authority, if it be granted that the revelation contained in the deposit of faith given to the Church is true. Authoritativeness, it might be argued—that is, the acknowledgment of authority—is not the foundation of authority. The authority of the magisterium descends to it from the truth, whether or not authoritativeness be accorded to it in return. Leadership may be desirable, but it pertains to the right exercise, not to the essential nature, of authority. For the teaching authority is established upon the truth, and this is received, not created, by the magisterium of the Church. The Church cannot therefore assume the authority required by the degree of initiative and creativity here suggested. The traditional concept of the teaching authority must be retained, precisely because the nature of Christian truth imposes stringent limitations upon the authority of the magisterium. The papal office, in particular, has no discretionary powers regarding the truth. It is, therefore, bound to express the truth as it is, whereas it is up to its listeners to disregard or to heed the magisterium's witness to the truth.

The adequacy of this view, however, depends upon what is meant by the truth. Perhaps we should briefly review certain points made above. The long tradition of Western philosophy has construed the mind as an instrument whereby men could acquire spiritually the perfection of other things. Accordingly, knowledge was the inward reduplication of outer reality, and truth was the conformity of the thinking mind to reality. The mind's true knowledge was then expressed outwardly through conventional signs: propositions embodied the truth insofar as they represented the mind's thinking, which in turn represented reality. This view, however, has gradually broken down, and the last century or so has witnessed the gradual emergence of a new way of understanding the mind and its truth. Though there is scarcely unanimity, there is significant convergence in philosophy towards the view that the human spirit is a self-creative process which fashions itself out of its relations to the world. If so, truth is that quality of consciousness that enables it to exist out of the past, beyond the present, projecting itself into the future. Creative thought has the quality of truth if, emerging from the past, it leads to further creative thought, if it opens up further possibilities for man's self-creation. Thus, truth is that quality of knowledge which accounts for the fact that the more we actually know, the more we potentially know: truth is the enlargement of the horizon of consciousness.

Of course, man's consciousness creates itself only out of its relationships to the real world, not out of its imagination. It is perfectly obvious, as I granted in an earlier chapter, that one cannot truthfully say or think whatever one wishes, regardless of the nature of the world in which one actually exists. Hence, it is true that true speech and true thought can be said to conform to things.

But this hardly means that knowledge is true *because* it conforms to reality, or that the truth of knowledge *consists* in its conformity with things. It is rather the other way about: if knowledge is true, then the mind could be said to conform to reality. The mind conforms to reality because it is true, that is, because it has the sort of knowledge that enables man to exist and develop in the real world. Likewise, to say that our speech is true because it states faithfully what happens in reality is to mistake the cause for the effect. Our speech is not true because it conforms to reality. On the contrary, if it makes any sense to say that language conforms to reality it is only because it has the quality of truth. For speech is not the outward representation of our prior, inner thinking about the world, but, on the contrary, the means whereby we think and relate ourselves to the world.

As long as we conceive the truth in the classical manner the teaching authority of the Church will be logically conceived as its entitlement to make certain statements to which assent should be given by the listener on account of their truth. From this it follows that the Church can teach authoritatively only that which is reducible to, or directly deducible from, the original truths or propositions which the Church was supposedly warranted to affirm. Conversely, concerning such matters the authority of the Church has nothing to do with the listener's disposition or reaction to its teaching. On the other hand, if we do not assume that truth is the conformity of the mind to things, but a quality of consciousness which only secondarily results in the relation of conformity to things, then the truth of the authoritative teaching is neither guaranteed by, nor restricted by its reducibility to, or by its deducibility from, propositions originally or traditionally affirmed by the Church. Indeed, if I may put it starkly, in the order of religion the Church has authority to teach anything whatever—as long as it is true. For if a teaching is true, then *it follows* that it will preserve, if not also enhance, the spirit of the original truth of every traditional doctrine of the faith. The continuity of the truth of the evolving doctrine of the faith is the continuity of the *truth* of the belief of the Church; it is not the continuity of the chain of deductions and explicitations from the earliest to the most recent pronouncement of the Church.

Surely no teaching is true *because* it conforms with tradition. Of course, it is tempting to rely on the principle that if the original teaching is true, then mere deduction and explicitation would appear to yield a necessarily true doctrine, if not also a sufficiently adequate one for all times. But, in point of fact, truth does not obey the laws of this sort of logical mechanism. Mere conformity to a true traditional teaching may under certain circumstances even betray the truth of that very tradition. For instance, the Church no longer insists on the accuracy of the process of creation according to Genesis. Why not? The reason is not that it considers the authority of human scientific reason to be superior to its own. The reason is that to insist upon it nowadays would be to *miss* the very point which Genesis presumably intends to teach, namely, a truth about man's relations to God. At one time this teaching could not have been imparted except in and through a cosmology. Today, on the contrary, it cannot be adequately taught except in abstraction from astrophysics and biology. Well, the magisterium has come to realize this in connection with specific issues such as Genesis—though this realization has usually come grudgingly and late. It has yet, however, to draw the general principle: to insist upon any given conceptual, culturally concrete form of religious truth, even after such a form has ceased to be consistent with the current form of man's cultural development, may be religiously prejudicial, precisely because it may *obscure* the very meaning which the obsolete conceptual form once *revealed*.

The overriding preoccupation of the magisterium with safe-keeping the original truth of the Catholic faith is surely unexceptionable and understandable—but it may be insufficient to that very end. The preservation of a certain number of traditional propositions does not necessarily ensure the adequacy of present teaching. And yet, the magisterium is immediately and above all responsible, not for the eternal adequacy of past teaching, but for the truth and adequacy of its present magisterial activities and their effect upon human beings. That is, the magisterium is bound to teach with as much truth and adequacy as it can derive from its own traditional spirit. To be sure, the magisterium of the Church must discern its own spirit, and it can do this only in the light of its own tradition. But the examination of the traditional teaching of the Church in order to discern its spirit need not suppose that the truth of the original doctrine lay in its originally faithful depiction of divine realities. In short, the authority of the magisterium of the Church is not a licence for commanding assent to certain propositions: it is a commission to cultivate the truth in the community of the Church and in the society of man.

Thus, it is true that the magisterium cannot measure the adequacy of its teaching by the pleasure or readiness with which it may be received. On the other hand, the authority of the magisterium cannot be divorced from the authoritativeness which it is accorded. The magisterium does not fulfill its teaching function responsibly if it imagines that its duties can be discharged by uttering eternal truths for the record, as it were, regardless of whether anyone listens, and irrespective of what listeners may think or do. In this connection I should mention that Pope Paul's evident reluctance to precipitate schism, and his refraining, to date, from issuing invitations to dissidents to leave the Church, bespeak a degree of wisdom and of genuine pastoral responsibility which, if persevered in, history is not likely to forget. On the other hand, one wishes that Pope Paul's sincere and unbounded concern for the truth of the Catholic faith were not allied with a philosophical concept of truth which, like every other, must be deemed in principle to be only historically valid and essentially apt to be improved upon.

The corollary of this conclusion is that the adequacy of the authoritative teaching of the Church today, and I have most specially in mind the teaching office of the Pope, depends at least as much on form as it does on content. Thus, the contemporary Pope might well not think of himself as benevolently commanding a flock of restive sheep, but as guiding men who, for all their moral and intellectual shortcomings, can fulfill their Christian vocations only to the degree that they themselves grow in consciousness, creativity and responsibility. The Church today needs the kind of papacy which would be distinguished not so much for its holy fatherhood as for its competent, politically wise, realistic and effective leadership.

6.

Man and God

In the last two chapters I have developed and illustrated the theme that the deep conflicts which mark the contemporary Catholic crisis begin with differences at the level of fundamental concepts and attitudes, particularly those which, like truth and reality, derive from a certain interpretation of the nature of language. In the first of these two chapters I suggested that this phenomenon is understandable, if it is true that faith is not distinguished from everyday experience because it covers a peculiar area of truth which would, supposedly, lie apart from the area of everyday experience, but rather because it is a peculiar quality of everyday experience, namely, that self-disposition which renders all experience meaningful and worthwhile. And I suggested that, therefore, it should be hardly surprising if one and the same faith should produce startlingly different doctrines, should the substratum of experience which faith renders meaningful be itself subject to development and change. I suggested, in other words, that as human nature evolves, and as human experience develops, one and the same faith—that is, one and the same response to the presence of the transcendent to human consciousness, one and the same commitment to the historical reality of God embodied in the Christian tradition—manifests itself in alternative doctrines and interpretations which, in a sense, are truly irreconcilable, truly incompatible, truly mutually exclusive—at least in what concerns content, though the spirit, of course, may remain the same. And I have implied that this situation is not so paradoxical as might appear at first sight; that, in fact, it makes a great deal of sense. But I have also explained the reason why, namely, that faith is not an imperfect sort of everyday consciousness about perfect and extraordinary matters, but that it is a distinct dimension of human experience which affects man's consciousness of all things. Religious faith is not unlike human love, whose constancy not infrequently leads to logical inconsistencies, and whose steadfastness would not always be obvious to him who should judge it by the simple-minded standard of *sic remanet, ut incepit.* If religious faith is transforming, and if it is a creative force, then it is scarcely extraordinary that the evolution of religious consciousness should show precisely the same characteristics which are found in biological evolution, namely, real creative novelty, real transformation, real irreducibility of the consequent to its antecedents, real difference between any given stage of development and the original one.

This is why, as I suggested in the last chapter, one and the same teaching authority of the Church may mean concretely different things at different times. The problem of the Church regarding the magisterium today is not that the hierarchical and papal government abuses its teaching authority but, on the contrary, that its teaching authority has been *de facto* largely abdicated by the government of the Church. The trappings of teaching have been, of course, retained. But a teaching that does not actually teach, a teaching whose very nature renders it unsuitable for learning, is hardly more than an empty form. By all means, let the magisterium continue to teach authoritatively. But may the magisterium first learn that it cannot possibly continue actually to teach simply by continuing to do as it has traditionally done whenever it intended to teach. For man has changed. The fundamental concepts, attitudes and modes of experience that define human nature have not remained the same with the passage of time. The doctrines of faith must change, not because faith was originally deficient or mistaken but, on the contrary, because to the extent that it was creative and true it has contributed to the development of human consciousness. Thus, the doctrines of faith must change because the nature of faith so requires; that is, the doctrines of faith must change because the human experience which faith makes meaningful and worthwhile does itself change—not least radically of all to the very degree that faith is an effective factor in the evolution of man.

In my exposition of this thesis, I have so far also assumed something else, a certain complementary view which I would now like to explore in a little more detail. And this is the view that the Christian faith is protean enough, catholic enough to give one and the same religious meaning and value to a variety of alternative forms of human experience—I mean, while remaining an identifiably Christian faith. In this final chapter I will attempt to illustrate this with reference to what I take to be among the most basic concepts of the Christian faith, namely, the concept of God.

Allow me to suggest, in the first place, that there is a serious problem concerning the compatibility of the traditional concept of God with the contemporary mode of experience. A few years ago a film entitled *On the Beach* was exhibited in this country and, as I watched it, it brought this problem home to me in a very forceful way. The theme of the picture was the throes of the human race as it died the slow death of radioactive poisoning in the wake of thermonuclear war. *On the Beach* was not a memorable example of cinematic art. Its portrayal of the variety of human reactions to the prospect of imminent and certain death was, as I thought, not very perceptive. In fact, I remember this picture mostly for a certain scene which appeared to me particularly inept. As the final days came to the remnant of mankind somewhere in Australia, and many were escaping into despair, madness and suicide, a Christian minister, (who was presumably only trying to help) prayed in behalf of his congregation: "Grant us, O Lord, as we enter our final days, the courage to accept Thy will."

I am not sure whether this prayer was intended to be ridiculous or shocking. Every indication given by the plot was that the fall-out which now threatened human life had been released, with full deliberation, by strictly human agents, without the intervention of exterminating angels or supernatural mishaps. Nevertheless, the implication of the prayer attributed to the Christian minister was that Christians should take consolation from the thought that the disaster must be somehow attributed ultimately to the will of God, resignation to which would be a source of reassurance for those who believed and hoped in Him.

Was this a misrepresentation of common Christian belief? I think not. It is common part of the Christian faith that if one believes in God one must also suppose that beyond mere human and natural causality stands the will, at least the permissive will, of God. The idea that the world as a whole is ordered and directed by God towards its final outcome seems to me scarcely foreign to belief in the Christian God. The minister I have quoted surely knew as well as you or I that fallout is only radioactive dust which rises up from earth before it rains down from above. But he probably also thought that unless God had permitted it not even the sinful will of man could have brought the catastrophe about. The scandal of reason was not that men should have caused it, but that the dreadful effects should have followed; not that men should have done it, but that God should have allowed it to happen at all. And so, this Christian minister tried to find meaning in the meaningless event, exhorting his people in the manner of Christians of all times. Though the death of mankind—for example—may seem on the face of it senseless, and to betray the indifference of God towards man, the true believer knows that it really indicates nothing òf the sort. In the mind of God the greatest evils, even the death of mankind, form part of a cosmic pattern which as a whole is intelligent and wise. Like Christians traditionally, the minister of *On the Beach* appeared to believe that although evil is real, somehow evil itself is turned by God to good account and made to contribute to the goodness of the universe as a whole.

Of course, Christians have long believed that God's Providence respects the freedom which is part of the human nature which God himself gave to man. Every individual is free to choose whether to incorporate himself to the will of God. But, as this tradition would say, if man so chooses, he co-operates with Divine Providence. If he chooses otherwise, however, he does not really frustrate God's will. All he achieves is his own undoing. He does not actually destroy the divine plan. For even man's free decisions against the will of God are foreseen and taken into account of by God. God's providential dispositions for creation as a whole, and for mankind as a whole, remain therefore in effect and cannot be thwarted. We may be certain that the outcome of the history of the world and of man will somehow fulfill the decrees of a Providential God.

Now, I suggest that if this way of thinking sounds ever more strange to many modern ears, the reason has to do at least in part with the evolution of human consciousness, and that it is doctrines like this which over the last century or two, as human culture has developed intensively, may have led many people actually to disbelieve in God. For many in our culture have come to think—or perhaps they have simply come to feel instinctively—that to believe in a God or this sort, or for that matter to believe in any God unconditionally and uncritically, regardless of what it should commit us to think and do, should offend the sense of propriety of any reasonable person of mature character and delicate moral sensibility. It is not that one should believe only in a God without mystery, a God totally open to human inspection. But one may not with a clear conscience believe in a God who is not consonant with human experience, and least of all in a God who outrages man's moral sense. The kind of God one believes in is, after all, the best measure of the depth of one's self-understanding and moral insight.

An articulate, if fictional, spokesman for this sort of agnosticism, which is born not out of indifference but, on the contrary, out of conscientious moral concern, is Jennet Jourdemayne, the heroine of Christopher Fry's *The Lady's not for Burning*. Condemned to the stake for her alleged unorthodoxy, Jennet is offered her life by one of her accusers, if only she will prostitute herself to him. She refuses. But her refusal is devoid of indignation. In fact, she is puzzled by her own decision to give up life, as they used to say, rather than virtue, and more to herself than to the villain she says:

> I am interested
> In my feelings. I seem to wish to have some importance
> In the play of time. If not,
> Then sad was my mother's pain, sad my breath,

132

Sad the articulation of my bones,
Sad, sad my alacritous web of nerves,
Woefully, woefully sad my wondering brain,
To be shaped and sharpened into such tendrils
Of anticipation, to feed the swamp of space.
What is deep, as love is deep, I'll have
Deeply. What is good, as love is good,
I'll have well. Then if time and space
Have any purpose, I shall belong to it.
If not, if all is a pretty fiction
To distract the cherubim and seraphim
Who so continually do cry, the least
I can do is to fill the curled shell of the world
With human deep-sea sound, and hold it to
The ear of God, until he has appetite
To taste our salt sorrow on his lips.
And so you see it might be better to die.
Though, on the other hand, I admit it might
Be immensely foolish.[1]

Perhaps one of the most significant developments—certainly one of the most surprising—in the history of Christian belief is the emergence in recent times of a not inconsiderable number of Christian believers, particularly among professional theologians, who share in many respects the very objections which in the past have moved many to agnosticism and atheism. Yet, though persuaded of the fundamental moral validity of the motives which in the past have led to disbelief, these Christians do not themselves disbelieve. The reason is that they are also convinced that the choice between belief and disbelief in the traditional concept of God is not a legitimate alternative. They think instead that the concept of God must, like every other, undergo development as man grows and matures. They believe that, as human conscious-

[1] (London, 1949), p. 85.

ness evolves, new possibilities for the evolution of the Christian faith are opened up. Their problem is, therefore, not how to defend the traditional concept of God against contemporary experience but, on the contrary, how to take advantage of the growth of human experience in order to improve upon their concept of God.

But to understand the meaning of these trends it is necessary first to recall that the Christian concept of a Providential God was born of the conjunction of two quite different ideas: one parent was Greek, the other Hebrew. The very name *Providence* is derived from *pronoia,* a Greek term meaning literally pre-intellection, that is, *pre-vision* or *fore-sight.* This concept was developed technically by the Stoics, a school of late Greek philosophy. But long before the Stoics, and indeed since the dawn of philosophical speculation, according to most Greek thinkers whatever happens happens necessarily. Events are intelligible only in the light of their necessary causes. (The very idea of science owes its origin to this belief.) Fate rules over all cosmic and human affairs.

According to the Stoics, however, fate should not be understood either in the naïve manner of mythology, that is, as a universal divine dispensation or as a discrete natural force vying with other natural forces, as had been supposed by other Greek philosophers. Fatefulness or necessity was not a single, separate principle or factor or universal law affecting the world: it was an intrinsic characteristic of the cosmos as a whole. Though any part of the cosmic process might not make sense by itself, the cosmic process as a whole must be supposed to be meaningful and to fulfill a purpose immanent in its very reality. Human wisdom is but the application of our finite reason to our finite decisions, so that our life will accommodate itself to the otherwise inscrutable purposes

134

of an infinitely wise nature. For if we struggle against fate we cannot but reap utter unhappiness. The prudent man submits instead to the inexorable nature of reality. Philosophy is the technique whereby man acquires knowledge and resignation, and thus happily adjusts to what is provided for him by the cosmos. The wise man learns to will that which will in any event come to pass.

Of course, man can fight the purposes of fate, but according to the Stoics this course is by definition doomed to defeat. However, though fate cannot be conquered, its unfortunate results for man can be, as it were, neutralized. Man can swim with the current of fate. He can genuinely will the inevitable, if only he can envisage it from the viewpoint of fate itself. This does not, of course, alter the inevitability of fate. But it reconciles man to his fate. And reconciliation to Fate is the only road to happiness.

The other component of the Christian idea of a Providential God comes from a more legitimate source. According to the Jewish tradition inherited by Christianity, God, who is the supreme reality, is not indifferent to human interests and feelings. On the contrary, God is man's friend. He is benevolent. Indeed, he actively seeks the welfare of man. Christian thinkers were thoroughly persuaded of this, and would have been incapable of looking upon existence with the baleful eye of the Greeks. Nevertheless, in much the same way as contemporary Christian thinkers inevitably and properly assume much of the scientific worldpicture of modern times, early Christian thinkers inevitably and properly assumed that the Stoic doctrine of Providence expressed a fundamental truth concerning the nature of intelligible reality. Hence, they did not reject Stoicism as a whole: they simply modified it wherever it seemed to conflict with their Christian faith. One of the results of this process was the transformation of the

Stoic doctrine of cosmic providence into the Christian doctrine of Divine Providence.

It was not difficult to achieve this. To the basic elements of the Stoic doctrine it was necessary for Christians merely to add the idea that the *logos,* or intrinsic rationality of the world, was not created, but divine. The *logos* was God himself, who created the world in accordance with his wisdom and who is personally interested in what happens in the world and most especially in what happens to man. By his Providence, therefore, God benevolently orders all things wisely, co-ordinating the natural finality of all things into the finality of creation as a whole. In this manner he fosters and infallibly achieves the good of the whole world, and in particular the good of man. This is why despite man's awareness of his own finitude and impotence, man need not fear for himself. If he believes in God, he can rest assured that his fate is in good, competent and friendly hands.

The difference between this and the Stoic concept of Providence is obvious. For instance, the attitude towards existence reflected by the Christian belief in Providence is largely optimistic and confident. But the Christian transformation of the Stoic *pronoia* did not alter every essential feature of Stoicism, particularly not in what pertains to the role of freedom in man's moral existence. Although the Christian concept of Providence did increase the sense of individual responsibility, for it enhanced the scope and effectiveness of human initiative required for the achievement of the destiny of the individual, the idea was retained that there was a real fate, a pre-ordained destiny of man. The reality of human freedom and the good will of God could not, as even Christians thought, take away the necessitation which alone makes reality intelligible and possible. However, predestination somehow did

136

not take away freedom or negate God's benevolence. But it never became at all clear precisely how this was so. The controversies of Pelagians, anti-Pelagians and semi-Pelagians were never fully resolved, and were bitterly renewed at the time of the Protestant Reformation. To this date Christianity, with but differences of emphasis among the major denominations, continues to assert both predestination and freedom in unstable balance and ineffective juxtaposition. It is fair to remark, however, that predestination has usually held the influential edge over freedom. For man's subjection to necessity has been practically self-evident to most Christian theologians, whereas the benevolence of God has been strictly a matter of religious faith.

But whereas, as I have said, regarding the individual the doctrine of Divine Providence did, for all its inadequacies, tend to increase man's sense of moral responsibility above the level permitted by Greek thought, regarding mankind as a whole the effect of the concept of Divine Providence was rather to confirm Christians in the Greek belief in historical determinism. Christians have tended to assume that moral responsibility accrues strictly to the individual, and that it bears upon the relations among individuals alone; it was only very slowly, and against the grain, that the Christian social consciousness awoke. Even then, Christian social concern has not gone much beyond recognition of the responsibility of individuals for contributing to the common good. The idea that man has a collective responsibility has been more or less consciously resisted. For collective responsibility implies collective freedom: it means that mankind as a whole is responsible for the social conditions that it creates. But, if so, no social system, no economic or political structure, no given form of the common good, can be said to be required by God's plan. There is, in short, no divinely established human order. This is a thought that Christianity has been unable to reconcile with its prior belief in the traditional Divine Providence—for it is indeed irreconcilable with such belief.

Moreover, mankind is not only a spatial collectivity. The human race is more than the totality of individuals existing on the surface of the earth at any given time. Man also is the historical collectivity of generations succeeding generations in time. If, on account of belief in Divine Providence as God's benevolent Fate, Christianity has neglected socio-political morality somewhat, it has almost completely ignored the historical dimensions of man's moral life. The idea that man is responsible for his own history has simply not been taken seriously by the Church. And thus, by default rather than by design, Christians have assumed that history can look after itself. Or, what is the same, that it is up to God to look after it. It is indeed not for us to presume to create the shape of things to come. Our task is to keep history on the right— that is, the divinely pre-set—time-track. For this reason Christians have not felt the need to take human evolution in hand, or to direct the course of historical events towards a consciously projected future time. We have, in other words, not really believed in heaven and hell as historical realities which can be brought about by the collective effort of man. For we have not so much as wondered whether history is, like individual men, creative and free. We have instead believed that history was fated by the Providence of God.

What some Christian thinkers have suggested with increasing insistence in modern times is, on the contrary, that belief in any form of fate, even in the benevolent fate of Divine Providence, is a distortion suffered by Christianity when its original belief was

138

cast in Greek terms. If God is not the Supreme Being of Greek philosophy, but the gratuitous, self-giving reality of the Gospel, then the ground on which God can claim worship from man is not his absolute power over creation, but the absolute openness of creation to receive within itself the gift of the presence of God. And what this in turn concretely means is that all history is possible. The shape of the world to come has not been determined beforehand, either by its own nature or by God's design. History is not subject to fate. There is no divine gimmicking of the inner works of creation so that events will come out in the end the way they were meant to from the outset. There is not so much as a sort of divine White Paper or prescription of principle concerning the general nature of the outcome of the world. There is, in brief, no divine plan: there cannot be such a plan if it is true that all history is truly possible and that, therefore, all history is truly free and that fate does not rule over human and cosmic affairs. This is why belief in the Christian God implies belief in the reality of heaven and hell.

For, given the reality of human freedom, then man's creation of history may well take place without, and even against, God. That is, man's real ability to create himself, and his real ability—given enough time—to create any possible world, mean that man, if he wants to, can create the sort of world in which there is no room for God, and the sort of history which dispenses with moral requirements transcending man himself. Well, the creation of such a world is what Christianity has traditionally called *sin,* and the outcome of such a history is what Christianity has traditionally called *hell.* It is clear that it is man, not God, who creates hell and establishes it, as it were, at the centre of the world. Metaphor aside, however, the point is that human history may well fail. The effort

139

of creation may well turn out to have been spent in vain. Such a failure is truly possible, that is, a real and eternal hell, a total cosmic failure is a real possibility, even if it has nothing to do with any kind of punishment willed by a jealous, angry or just God. The definitive and utter bankruptcy of the human enterprise may well be the result of history as a whole: this is a thought Christians cannot easily entertain, this is a possibility we do not easily admit.

Of course, the Christian hope is that this real possibility will not, in fact, come to pass, because man will instead accept the presence and reality of God. For although there is, according to Christian belief, no fate which necessitates the ultimate success of man, there is none to forbid it either. On the contrary, man is invited, he is called, precisely to bring about the positive achievement of history. Whether or not we may wish to call this achievement the "victory" of God is irrelevant. The point is that the ultimate and total achievement of history is believed by Christians to be perfectly possible too, an achievement which in the Judaeo-Christian tradition is metaphorically known as the Kingdom of God. The Kingdom of God, or heaven, is the outcome of history when history is created by man in the presence of God.

The trend of thought I have been illustrating here, the opinion that belief in God need not imply that God fulfills, albeit benevolently, the same function that the Greeks ascribed to blind fate—this trend of thought logically leads to the view that the traditional Christian concept should be revised, above all regarding God's relation to history and time. This is why some Christian philosophers and theologians in recent times have further suggested that God's role in creation is not that of directing and guiding history from afar towards an appointed end, but that of

140

being present to it as man creatively invents it, and thus invents himself. If so, the unfolding of human life should not be thought of as barred by riddles spun by a divine sphinx: which alternative is really in accordance with the will of God? Instead, moral problems should be conceived as the challenge of the presence and self-manifestation of God to man, inviting man to surpass himself and to fashion his own future, as he would a ladder whereby to ascend unto the very reality of God.

Somewhat the same idea might be put in converse terms. To be aware of man's freedom, to believe that man is in no way subject to fate, is to conceive man in terms of responsibility for himself: it is to be committed to the idea that man's historical creativity makes him responsible for his own individual and collective outcome. Well, to believe in God is to believe that the self-creation of man is not automatically successful simply because it occurs—any more than it should be deemed impossible simply because man's need willy-nilly to create himself is not optional, but is part of the situation in which man becomes aware of himself. To believe in God is to believe that the final assessment of individual and collective human creativity is not arrived at either by man measuring history by his own standard, or by God according to divinely pre-destined norms. For God's judgment does not consist in measuring off one reality against another, to which the first is required to conform. The outcome of life and history is judged precisely as a free and imaginative creation which obeys no pre-established plan. The Gospel parable of the talents might be profitably recalled at this point in order to illumine the concept of God as present to a self-creative human nature that becomes conscious of itself as existing within a process of cosmic evolution which manifests itself to man as historical freedom. Hence, to believe in God is to be-

141

lieve that human progress is neither inevitable nor impossible, and that the human enterprise is neither doomed to fail nor destined to succeed. The future is truly open to achievement. And that which stands in the openness of the future is what we may by another name call God.

Now, I began this discussion with the stated purpose of illustrating the thesis that the Christian faith is protean enough, catholic enough to give one and the same meaning to a variety of alternative forms of human experience. I leave it up to you to decide whether I have made my point. But let me make very clear the standards by which I would prefer that you decide. The argument I have presented is *not* that recent theological speculation about God must be granted the right to exist because it attempts to express the traditional Christian faith in a manner suitable for our time, and that the evident continuity between such speculation and the constant tradition guarantees such right to exist. My point is rather the opposite: that surely the essentially pluriform character of the Christian faith is more clearly illustrated by the traditional theologies than by the most daring suggestions of later times. For, surely, if the concept of God which begins with the Old Testament and which is preached and developed in the Gospel and which is best summed up in John's doctrine of charity —if such a concept of God could once make meaningful the thoroughly alien attitude towards reality, the pessimistic and tragic orientation of human life embodied in the Greek concept of Fate, and most particularly in the Stoic concept of Providence, then there could be no reasonable doubt that it could make meaningful all imaginable forms which human experience could possibly take. If, I say, the Christian faith could absorb, transform and redeem even the idea of Providence, then it could surely absorb, transform and redeem any other idea whatever, as it is difficult to conceive a greater contradiction than between, on the one hand, freedom and charity, and, on the other, necessity and fate.

In any event, perhaps you will now understand why to some people today, even to some Christians, the prayer of the minister of *On the Beach* would sound scandalous, repellent and indicative of no nobler religious feeling than irresponsibility. For least of all in the face of mankind's self-inflicted death should we pray for resignation to God's will, when more to the point might be to pray for insight and resolve. Now, consider the present moment in the evolutionary history of man. We are not yet "on the beach"; in our flight from reason we have not reached the point of no return. But we can already foresee that the present course of our human affairs can lead mankind only to ultimate self-destruction. May we suppose, then, for instance, that the problem of political ethics today is to determine which nation, which ideology, which disputant, must be deemed to act, if not in whole at least in predominant part, in accordance with the will of God? The very posing of the problem in such terms assumes an immoral degree of resignation to a situation (presumed to be neither man's responsibility nor under his control) in which, for example, thermonuclear war is thought to be a possibly legitimate option at least for those who have the margin of justice on their side. On the contrary, the real problem is how to change the options themselves, closing some off and opening up new ones. The real question is no longer whether war can be just, but whether it is morally permissible for man to fail to change the world and reshape history in such a manner that the dilemmas of the past shall not arise. The true scandal of reason is not that dreadful

143

effects should follow from evil, but that men should cause evil to occur; not that God should permit natural or moral catastrophes to happen, but that we should try to do nothing about the former, and that we should bring the latter upon ourselves.

War is, of course, only an example. Moreover, the task of self-creation is not only negative, how to avoid coming to a bad end, but positive, how to design the future and how to make it come to pass. The Christian re-conceptualization of God regarding such aspects as Divine Providence may help heighten man's conscience to the level of responsibility currently required of him. If so, Christians may yet make a signal contribution to the next stage of human evolution, encouraging man to multiply his creativity, and helping him determine what sort of future he should bring about. But Christians of this stamp would, of course, no longer expect the mere passage of time to fulfill God's providential plan. For they would believe instead that unless man dreams it up and makes it be, Heaven shall never come to pass, and that unless they die and are raised up to God, Eternal Life shall never begin.

Philosophy and the Limitations of Renewal

It is a corollary of the theses I have elaborated in the course of these lectures that the relevance of Catholic Christianity to the immediate as well as to the long-term future development of man depends very largely on the adequacy of the new philosophical orientation that Catholicism may decide to take today. Of course, not every possible new orientation would be as adequate as every other, and he would be a very sanguine seer who thought he could discern the difference with any great degree of certitude. However, it does not take an unusual amount of wisdom, only some realism and historical sense, to develop the moral conviction that, whatever else should define it, the orientation of Catholic philosophy today must be new. Catholic philosophical traditionalism has all but gone to its eternal reward in the Heaven of the history of Christian thought, and the Catholic community knows it. Even traditionalists, for all their whistling in the dark, do in the daylight of their solar plexus know it. There is no likelihood whatever, so far as I can estimate, that it will survive —at least not in its unreconstructed form.

145

But *there* is the problem and the snare. The demise of the long-established type of Thomism should be hardly a cause for rejoicing if its spirit should prove to be a phoenix and should manage to rise again in a new body of philosophical propositions which would be all the more unequal to the historical needs of contemporary Christianity because their updated style and their apparent novelty lulled the Catholic community into the opinion that the repristination of belief (as contrasted with its evolutionary development) was enough and, indeed, the upper acceptable limit of change for the Christian faith today. By these allusions I refer to that pluriform but plainly recognizable movement sometimes known as Transcendental Thomism, which I have elsewhere criticized as a whole.[1] But on this occasion I have especially in mind that sort of Transcendental Thomism which, under the leadership of Bernard Lonergan, makes North America its habitat.

It will not surprise the reader of this book to learn that in my opinion it would be best if Catholic thought did not remain content with the philosophical principles which spell the limitations of "renewal." But above all it is important that the Catholic community fully critically assess the fundamental options open to it. If it should wish to retain the classical epistemological and metaphysical premises and simply repair the conclusions they support, it is its privilege to do so. But it should do so, if at all, only aforethought, conscious of the nature and import of its decision, not on the basis of a vague hope that a duly restored Thomism of novel denomination will furnish Christian reform without tears, or that it will incorporate to itself all that is rele-

[1] *The Foundations of Belief,* Appendix II, "On Transcendental Thomism," pp. 499–522.

vant, true and valuable in contemporary philosophical thought.

In my suggestion, on the contrary, the evolution of Christianity will have painfully to reach the depths of the Christian soul: it will be no less radical and wrenching a process than any other conversion. And the philosophy of Lonergan, as I shall try to show in this essay, is vulnerable to the criticism that it proceeds strictly within the limitations of the Hellenic-Western epistemological and metaphysical tradition, even after the development of that very tradition has indicated the advisability, and created the possibility, of transcending those limitations. As for these limitations, I may summarily define them as (a) the assumption that cognition relates things (namely, man and world, or mind and object, or self and non-self, or even act and content) which were originally, prior to knowledge, unrelated, and (b) the assumption that the real, as such and in itself, is constituted by its intelligibility, that is, by its aptitude for entering into relation with a mind—and specifically by its aptitude for being the formal cause of that relationship which is the truth of the intellect that understands it.

Of course, in the fairly long history of Greek-Western speculation these assumptions have undergirded quite diverse epistemologies and metaphysics. Not every criticism applicable to, for instance, Plato is necessarily applicable to Aristotle or to St. Thomas—nor is every criticism validly made of the latter two also validly made of, say, Lonergan. On the other hand, Plato and St. Thomas, Aristotle and Descartes, Kant and Gilson, Hegel and Maritain, differ only within the limits of their common ground of agreement. Likewise with Lonergan and them. I am concerned with that which is common to the entire tradition of which Lonergan is a member, and I refer not to what distin-

147

guishes him from, but to that which binds him to, that tradition.[2] Hence, it is not particularly relevant to present purposes that, to begin at the beginning, Lonergan's epistemology may well be distinguishable from naïve realism, or from the somewhat more sophisticated realism of, say, a Gilson.[3] It is not particularly relevant, that is, if Lonergan's epistemology is nevertheless some sort of realism, and if Lonergan finds no alternative to every form of idealism except some form of realism.

[2] My being concerned with it is in part a reflection of the fact that I, too, stand in the same tradition. On the other hand, I understand myself as diverging from that tradition at the very level at which Lonergan remains bound to it. Apprehending thus the evolutionary, historical nature of philosophical (and indeed all) enquiry, I conclude that further philosophical reflection is most likely (in fact, it is certain) to show that one may diverge from the Hellenic-Western tradition at a level such as I diverge from, and still remain bound to it at a yet more fundamental level which remains to be critically extricated and diverged from. There is nothing unusual in this conclusion. It amounts, as I have said, but to the recognition of the historicity of philosophical (and all other) reflection. It is but the realization that philosophy (and all human consciousness generally) evolves continuously, without discontinuities or gaps.

[3] However, the question might be more profitably raised whether it differs so very much from the doctrine of Maritain. Students of Lonergan appear sometimes to assume that Lonergan's criticism of Gilson automatically applies to Maritain. Even *prima facie* this would be most unlikely, given the extremely restricted scope of Gilson's epistemological work and Maritain's lifetime preoccupation with it. Now, I know of no reason why Lonergan should be compelled to take account of the doctrine of Maritain. But students of Lonergan have sometimes dismissed Maritain (and not merely ignored him, as they were entitled to do) on the ground that Lonergan has as effectively demolished Maritain as he has Gilson. Since I am not a Lonergan scholar I cannot say with certainty that this is not the case. But from my limited acquaintance with Lonergan's writings, this accomplishment, (the real possibility of which I have yet to be convinced of), is in any event not one which has yet taken place. And I doubt even the possibility of it neither because I question Lonergan's capacity nor Maritain's vulnerability, but because I detect far too great a similarily between Maritain and Lonergan at key epistemological points.

148

Therefore, Lonergan may well denounce "the nonsense of naïve realism, of the super-look that looks at both the looking and the looked-at." [4] And he may well insist that he "place[s] transcendence, not in going beyond a known knower, but in heading for being." [5] And he may well explain that "our intellects are not a second sense, they do not look." [6] It remains—at least, if I apprehend his intention correctly—that, in Lonergan's view, when the intellect actually understands, the intellect becomes identical with the intelligible in act; indeed, it becomes the intelligible in act. Hence, it matters little that "the union of object and subject is a metaphysical deduction from the fact of knowledge" [7] rather than a self-evident datum of consciousness. For, in any event, cognition remains a union, indeed a unification, or knower and known, of man and world, insofar as cognition essentially consists in the overcoming of an original metaphysical isolation of man and the world.

Of course, in Lonergan's thought cognition may not be a union or even a unification in the sense that out of two original realities a single third reality—the intellect in act—subsequently results. All but the least sophisticated living Thomists are well aware that the actuality of knowledge pertains to the knower alone, and that this so-called "union" of knowledge is, as it were, a strictly *unilateral* union, in which the totality of the change accrues to the knower alone. And at least some living Thomists other than Lonergan and his fellow transcendental Thomists also

---

[4] "The dehellenization of dogma," in *The Future of Belief Debate,* ed. Gregory Baum, (New York, 1967), 69–91; p. 73. (Henceforth cited as *Debate.*)

[5] *Insight,* (London, 1958), p. 377.

[6] "Consciousness and the Trinity," p. 6.

[7] *Debate,* p. 73.

realize that the important point here is that cognition consists in the knower's acquisition of a perfection found originally only in another and, thus, in the knower's overcoming of an original absence of perfection in himself. Let us say, then, in order to stress the point, that the overcoming of the original isolation of knower and known takes place strictly in the knower, so that the known's isolation survives the event of cognition and persists even after the knower's overcoming of *his* metaphysical isolation from the known. That is, let us say that the union of knower and known, the knower's act of possessing (by virtue of the very *esse* of the operation of knowledge) the perfection of another, is a union only in the sense that, whereas prior to knowledge the knower lacks that perfection, when the knower is in act he actually has that perfection—and, indeed, has it as part of *his* reality and being. For it is precisely its having become *his* perfection that warrants the definition of knowledge as "becoming *the other* as other." Cognition may not be well described as "becoming *one* with the other"; this is true. But the reason is not that cognition is no union at all, but rather, as another Thomist has put it, that the knower is "incomparably more *one* with the known than matter with form." [8] In sum, Lonergan may well avoid the terminology of other Thomists and prefer his own, such as "heading for being"—a terminology which, of course, for all its possible advantages does not enjoy the impossible privilege of having no disadvantages of its own. But Lonergan retains the basic idea just the same. If "transcendence [is] . . . heading for being," transcendence is the negation of immanence. Knowledge is the overcoming of the immanence of the substantial, subjective reality of man.

[8] Jacques Maritain, *Les degrés du savoir,* (Paris, 1948), p. 218.

Of course, it may well be that I misunderstand Lonergan, and that he does *not* effectively conceive knowledge in this way at all. In that case I would have to reappraise my appraisal of Lonergan —wondering all the while why he had not stated the point more clearly, or how he could nevertheless deem that he reproduced without essential change the doctrine of St. Thomas. But I imagine there is little likelihood of my having to wonder about these things. For the indications abound that I have not radically misunderstood him in this respect. To search for evidence I have to go no further than, for instance, to Lonergan's positing the "pure desire to know," a spontaneous inclination built into the nature of the intelligent creature, the principle whereby it can overcome its metaphysical isolation from the world.

To explain how the doctrine of the "pure desire to know" corroborates my contention, (namely, that Lonergan abides by the traditional assumptions concerning the nature of knowledge), I should first amplify a point I have already made. The direct antecedent of the traditional view, that the essential aspect of knowledge is the subject's transcendence of his subjectivity, is the doctrine that every being as such is unrelated to, isolated, separated off from, every other. St. Thomas' peculiar variation of this typically Greek doctrine consists in locating the ground of this metaphysical atomism, as it were, in the very act of existence of being: St. Thomas' great distinction, as one might put it, is to have transmuted metaphysical atomism into existential monadism. In any event, the doctrine is most clearly explained by St. Thomas in a well-known text which explicitly connects it with the nature of knowledge: "Since the specific act of existence of one thing is distinct from the specific act of existence of another, in every created thing of this kind the perfection falls short of absolute perfection to the extent that that perfection is found in other species. Consequently, the perfection of each individual thing considered in itself is imperfect, being a part of the perfection of the entire universe, which arises from the sum total of the perfections of all individual things. In order that there might be some remedy for this imperfection, another kind of perfection is to be found in created things. It consists in this, that the perfection belonging to one thing is found in another. This is the perfection of the knower insofar as he knows; for something is known by the knower by reason of the fact that the thing known is, in some fashion, in the possession of the knower." [9]

In other words, knowledge is, from a certain perspective, a being's (intentional) possession of the perfection of another, over and above his own (entitative) perfection; it is "becoming the other as such." From a yet more formal perspective, however, and considering not so much the finality or the operation of knowledge but its formal *ratio* in the metaphysical order, we must say that this "becoming the other as other" is the knowing being's transcending of his own immanence; it is the knowing being's overcoming of his own in-itselfness, his own self-identity; it is the knowing being's transcendence of the limitations imposed upon it by its own existence; it is, if you will, "heading for being." For every being as such is isolated, by its very being, from every other being. Well, cognition is the (intentional, or even spiritual) overcoming of this isolation in the order of *being*.

But this means that the pre-cognitive isolation of being as such could be overcome only if there were a pre-cognitive principle within every knowing being which could function as the ground

[9] *De Veritate*, II, 2.

of overcoming such isolation. For the isolation in question is of the order of being—hence it is total and absolute. The ultimate and most formal principle of knowledge, whereby the metaphysical isolation of the knower can be overcome, cannot be anything in the known; it cannot be anything in "the other," because by being in "the other" it is therefore effectively cut off, totally and absolutely, from the knower. It must therefore reside in the knower himself. It must be an *immanent* principle of transcendence, as it were. Thus, it must be concluded that there is in the intellect an intrinsic principle of knowledge which "is neither ignorance nor knowledge, but the dynamic intermediary between ignorance and knowledge."[10] This is a sort of predisposition to know. But it must be distinguished, for instance, from the ordinary predisposition to know—curiosity, if you will—which follows upon prior knowledge, for we are dealing now with the absolutely first principle of knowledge, prior to which there is no knowledge at all. Let us therefore call it, as Lonergan does, the "pure" desire to know.

The point I am driving at is that the presupposition underlying Lonergan's doctrine of the "pure desire to know"—which strikes me as a rather central aspect of his epistemology—without which presupposition there would be scarcely any *raison d'etre* for the doctrine, is precisely the classical idea that knowledge is the overcoming of the isolation of the knower from his world. As for my suspicion that the doctrine of the "pure desire to know" is of more than passing importance to Lonergan's thought, perhaps I could best substantiate this by recalling that the "pure desire to know" is the origin of, indeed it is identical with, the "notion" (as contrasted with the "concept") of being. In Loner-

[10] "Natural knowledge of God," p. 8.

gan's own words, "the notion of being is the desire to understand what is prior to understanding anything." [11] All human understanding stems from the pure desire to know. And the understanding of understanding, like the understanding of being as such, may be successfully undertaken only to the extent that we develop the method for arriving at such understanding from our prior understanding of the implications of the pure desire to know.

Evidently, Lonergan's doctrine of the "pure desire to know" and of the "notion of being" is distinguishable from, say, Descartes' doctrine of innate ideas, as well as from Augustine's doctrine of illumination—just as Aristotle's doctrine of the agent intellect is distinguishable from Plato's doctrine of anamnesis, and Leibniz's doctrine of pre-established harmony from Hegel's doctrine of the Absolute Spirit. But, like Descartes and Augustine, Hegel and Plato, Leibniz and Aristotle, Lonergan needs a principle whereby the pure potency to understand becomes actually understanding. The reason, in each of these, is that knowledge is the overcoming of the irreducible metaphysical separation and un-relation of every being as such from every other being as such. This is why I would conclude as follows. Insofar as the transcending of the metaphysical separation, un-relation or isolation between man and his world may be fittingly called the introduction of unity between knower and know, the concept of knowledge common to the Greek-Western philosophical tradition may well be called the concept of knowledge as *unification* or, if you will, as transcendental identity. And insofar as this concept of knowledge achieves the knower's possession of the perfection of another, or the transcendence of the knower's in-itselfness, it may well be

[11] "Consciousness and the Trinity," p. 6

also called the concept of knowledge as *reduplication* or, if you will, as transcendental assimilation. For all his differences from other philosophers in this tradition, Lonergan—at least, so far as I understand him—appears to think of cognition in fundamentally the same way as they do, that is, as unitive and reduplicative.

Of course, to show that Lonergan shares common premises with the epistemological tradition which comes down from the Greeks to our own day is not to show that Lonergan is mistaken. The inadequacies of that tradition would have to be independently demonstrated. I have elsewhere explained in some detail, however, and at much greater length than the present occasion would permit, why it appears to me a fairly sound opinion that the traditional concept of knowledge is no longer rationally tenable. That is, although it is not a total and absolute error, it is nevertheless insufficient and must be thoroughly revised, (possibly along the lines I have also suggested at yet greater length). I will therefore but allude summarily to the two principal sources of my dissatisfaction with the epistemological bases of Lonergan's thought.

The first is that the history of philosophy reveals the impossible consequences of this view of knowledge; it reveals, that is, why a viable theory of knowledge is ultimately impossible once knowledge is conceived in the manner I have described. However, though history reveals its ultimate absurdity, it also reveals at the same time its original plausibility and the grounds of its supersession.

No doubt, the history of philosophy may be read differently by different people—and I know of no final court of arbitration which could settle once for all disputes in this, any more than in any other, area of scholarship. On the other hand, Lonergan's reading of the history of philosophy appears to me exceedingly inadequate, not because his interpretation of it is thoroughly at variance with mine (for I try to avoid using the presumed truth of my views as the standard whereby to judge the validity of someone else's), but because the very procedure which he appears to employ seems to me effectively to deny the historicity of the history of philosophy. So far as I can judge, Lonergan assumes that the truth of the thought of St. Thomas is privileged with ahistorical qualities—(for instance, though Thomisn may develop, in the sense that it may be improved upon, it does not evolve or take its place within the history of all human knowledge as one among many undetermined, unnecessitated and unnecessary stages in the development of human understanding). And it is not only that Lonergan apparently judges all enquiry, including history, to have an ahistorical and acultural reality, since "the methodology of history is not quite historic (while the history of the methodology of history would be a historical question, the methodology of history itself is not historic)." [12] It is above all that, accordingly, Lonergan does not situate *himself* historically within the philosophical tradition that leads to our own day.

He does situate himself, of course, in continuity with St. Thomas—but he does this as if Descartes, Kant, Hegel, Heidegger

[12] "Notes from the introductory lecture in the philosophy of history," p. 1. The reason is, of course, the essentially ahistorical, acultural and, therefore, *eternal,* character of truth. On the other hand, according to Lonergan, since the human mind exists in time, the eternal truth of, for instance, philosophy, is temporalized or historicized in the human mind: "the presentation of a subject at the present time is, briefly, four dimensional and philosophy is no exception" (*ibid.*, p. 14). This does not mean, however, that historicity is of the essence of science, but simply that science can become historicized: "the development of the presentation of any science, or any subject at the present time, has a historical dimension, we've become historicized. 'Truth is eternal in an eternal mind,' according to St. Thomas; and our minds are not eternal" (*ibid.*, p. 14).

and Sartre were not also historically continuous with St. Thomas, or as if their philosophies did not throw light upon the inward logical dynamic of the entire Greek-Western tradition and therefore upon St. Thomas himself—and, thus, as if they, unlike St. Thomas, need not be incorporated into any contemporary philosophical synthesis, but only sacked and spoiled in its favour, or else corrected and amended by it. In short, the history of philosophy appears to have taught Lonergan but the lesson that the doctrine of St. Thomas may be perfected. For instance, it teaches how the transcendental method devised (or was it come across, *discovered*?) by St. Thomas, but imperfectly realized by him, was explicitated, to our benefit, by Kant. But the history of philosophy does not appear to have taught Lonergan the far more important lesson that philosophy is historical in nature, and that therefore to philosophize without deriving one's orientation from the history of philosophy is like attempting to cross the Atlantic in overcast weather without a compass: one will, without a doubt, do a great deal of sailing, but the success of the trip will be far from assured.

For, if I may belabour the point, being in history—rather, awakening to find that one is already in history—is much like suddenly finding oneself in the centre of a sunless ocean or in the middle of a cosmic woods without being able immediately to recall how one got there. There would be no point in trying to get away from it altogether in order to get somewhere, because there is nowhere outside the ocean of being or the forest of the world. On the other hand, there is the forest itself to be explored. If one is to go on living, one must make the woods one's abode. But to be lost in the woods of time, or be unaware of the location of one's goal, is not at all to be uncertain as to where one is. For *one* is always "here." When we say *we* are lost we allow our language

157

to betray us. It is never *we* who are lost. What may be lost is one's home. What we may be unable to find is our chosen goal. We do not lose ourselves, we lose our way. But if all we know is that we are here, without knowing where elsewhere is, we cannot find our way, that is, we remain unaware of the direction in which we must strike in order to get somewhere else. Without orientation we can only ramble—or else remain bound to the vicinity, pretending that the world stops at the horizon. In any event, we would be getting nowhere.

The metaphor may be homely, but the moral, I hope, will be useful nonetheless. Unless the philosopher consciously locates himself within the past he will not be in a position consciously to create the future. Lonergan does not even attempt to orient himself historically—except perhaps as a disciple of St. Thomas. But discipleship—whether to St. Thomas or to Ayer and Ryle—is the denial of the historicity of philosophy. Lonergan has, to my mind, the same difficulty as, say, linguistic analysts do: assuming that only philosophers stand in history, but that philosophy itself, or the philosophical method, does not, they must passively and even unconsciously undergo the moulding forces of history and forgo the possibility of influencing the conscious, free development of history in their turn. If Lonergan interpreted the history of philosophy historically—and I repeat, it is not so much that he attempts to interpret it historically, but does so incorrectly, it is that he does not appear even to try—he might find that it is scarcely enough, in order to philosophize today, to try to avoid, on the basis of St. Thomas' thought, all the epistemological difficulties that have been raised since Descartes precisely on the basis of St. Thomas' thought. He might even conclude that it is imperative to reinterpret the very empirical data on which the metaphysical tradition before St. Thomas had been originally erected. In sum, my first criticism of Lonergan's epistemology is that, unaware of the historicity of philosophy, Lonergan fails to question critically the most basic assumptions of the Hellenic-Western epistemological tradition within which he, as a matter of fact, philosophizes and exists.

This is, therefore, a criticism of his procedure. My second criticism deals with substance. It is that Lonergan, handicapped by an insufficiently historical perspective and, therefore, by an insufficiently critical method, fails to realize what the Hellenic-Western philosophical tradition which reaches to our own day is now in a position to begin to realize, namely, that the analysis of consciousness yields the same conclusion as does the analysis of the history of the analysis of consciousness: cognition is not a replication, it is not the overcoming of the knower's isolation from his world. Knowledge is not the conquest of the limitations of self-containment and self-sufficiency; it is a separation which differentiates what is self-contained and self-sufficient out of what is not so; it is not the reduplication of another, but the creation of oneself. Of course, I do not claim that this view of knowledge is so self-evident, so far above all reasonable criticism, that it may be used as a criterion whereby the truth or falsity of an alternative view, such as Lonergan's, might be determined *a priori*. I do suggest, however, that if one first reaches this conclusion, as I have, on independent grounds and in the light of the evidence I have set out elsewhere, one will therefore find it necessary, as I do, if I may apply to Lonergan the same categories that Frederick Crowe has applied to me, to disagree with Lonergan at the fundamental level of his "main project," however valuable one might judge or surmise the "related developments" to be. As for my positive reasons for this conclusion, I will return to the matter below, in connection with my criticism of Lonergan's views on language and truth.

Meanwhile I will remark that, once a philosopher embarks upon the epistemological route followed by Lonergan, he cannot very well avoid arriving at the metaphysical thicket to which the path, of its own nature, leads. For once a philosopher conceptualizes man's transcendence as "heading for being" he can hardly fail to draw the implication that being is what man's transcendence heads for. If Parmenides may be fittingly called the father of metaphysics, it is because he appears to have been the first philosopher in our tradition to have realized this. But I do not believe it is necessary to survey Lonergan's work exhaustively, or to analyze his philosophy minutely, in order to judge that he repeats the reasoning of Parmenides and arrives at the same view. The real, Lonergan says—and I presume he says it *formaliter loquendo*—is "what is known by a true affirmation . . . the real [is] what you know when you truly affirm." [13] Conversely, affirmability by an act of true knowledge—that is, by a judgment—is what defines the real as such. And since what is affirmed by such an act is what any reality really *is,* it may also be said (indeed, it may be unquestioningly and unquestionably assumed) that the real as such is being as such. Hence, being as such is intelligible, that is, its nature is to be intelligible: "everything is intelligible . . . even prime matter, though not in itself, but in its form." [14] It also follows, may I add incidentally, that infinite being, or being in full act, is infinitely intelligible. Indeed, perhaps it should be put the other way about: if there is infinite being, it is

[13] "The origins of Christian realism," p. 7.
[14] "Consciousness and the Trinity," p. 7.

only because it is infinitely intelligible. That is, "the intelligible is the sort of thing that to be in full act is to be infinite." [15]

But it is supererogatory to collect evidence in support of this point when Lonergan openly avows his adherence to the Principle of Parmenides, "that which can be and that which can be thought are the same." For in reply to the suggestion that this principle may be superseded Lonergan has flatly stated: "Parmenides' identity still stands." [16] Just as above, with reference to Lonergan's adherence to the traditional concept of knowledge, Lonergan's admission of his adherence to the Principle of Parmenides does not constitute an infallible criterion whereby Lonergan's philosophy can be evaluated *a priori*. It does mean, however, that there would be little purpose served by evaluating Lonergan's elaboration of the metaphysical insight of the long philosophical tradition that began with Parmenides unless the adequacy of that insight were first assumed. And it does mean, moreover, that if one has independently concluded that the Principle of Parmenides is inadequate one will not find it possible to grant otherwise to Lonergan simply on his flat reassertion of that Principle, or on the ground of its presumed self-evidence, or by reason of its supposed indispensability to philosophical thought. It means, in short, that however elevated one's appreciation of the value of Lonergan's contribution to the Hellenic-Western tradition may be, one will not necessarily wish to share his unquestioning commitment to the perpetuation, rather than to the transcendence, of that tradition.

As I have explained in my own work, I cannot accept the Principle of Parmenides because (a) it is inherently incredible, if

[15] *Ibid.*, p. 7.
[16] *Debate*, p. 87.

not indeed superstitious, and (b) its incredibility, or at very least the absence of empirical evidence in its favour, is not overcome by the basic argument which can be adduced in its behalf, namely, that unless it is posited, the Greek (or, if you wish, the Greek-Christian) view of truth cannot be upheld. For I have no vested interest in the Greek-Christian traditional view of truth. On the contrary, if I might speak now in a very personal vein, I should say that, far from a vested interest, my spontaneous inclination would definitely bespeak a bias against it. Now, I hope I remain sufficiently devoted to the truth that I would not allow this inclination to dictate my conclusions. But I acknowledge such a bias as a matter of fact—just as I acknowledge as a matter of fact that my religious convictions are partly responsible for it. For, being a plain, though modern Christian (that is, a Christian who does not believe that to be a Christian one must also think as a Greek, and one who believes instead that the only sensible way to be a Christian today is to admit the reality of the present day), I am disinclined to believe in the hidden power of the immanent divinities which, as Thales thought, all things are full of. Belief in the Christian God implies, so far as I am concerned, a positive disbelief in Fate: necessity be damned, for all I care. I refuse— let me make the religious nature of this act of un-faith clear, I refuse—until, if ever, I should be shown otherwise, to believe the primitive superstitions that there are implicit necessities within being, that being has, as its very reality, an inner warrant to command assent, and that invisible predeterminations constitute it and make it definable as that which has an antecedent call on the intellect.

The faith of this dis-belief is not, of course, a source of apodictic certainty. But I find it liberating nonetheless, as it renders cogent

162

an otherwise paradoxical thought: it is one's very devotion to the truth that should permit one to call all truth into question. It is, thus, my very interest in the truth of my understanding of the nature of truth that allows me to examine critically and to put to the test of doubt every way of understanding the nature of truth. Hence, my way of envisaging the truth is, as I would willingly admit, not necessarily correct. But one of its advantages over Lonergan's is precisely that I can put it into question as easily as I can put Lonergan's, whereas Lonergan can actually question neither his view of truth—nor even mine. That he cannot question his view of truth is clear, since he needs his (self-evident) view of truth, as he believes, in order to *assert* his (self-validating) view of truth. But, if this be so, he cannot really question mine either, because his view of truth requires him to measure the validity of my view of truth by the criterion of his own. He cannot criticize any view of truth from within, or *a posteriori*, but only by the standard whether such a view of truth corroborates his own. Lonergan can state flatly, of course, that someone else's understanding of truth—for instance, mine—is incorrect. But all he can mean by this is that it is incompatible with his own. Therefore, he can scarcely avoid the trap that this represents, namely, dogmatism. In the last analysis, then, my criticism of Lonergan is none other than that which has been frequently levelled at metaphysical thought: that it confuses self-consistency with validity, that it cannot avoid self-encirclement into apriorism and circularity, and that therefore its contribution to the development of human understanding is impaired by the danger of its ultimate degeneration into dogmatism. Allow me to explain this at greater length.

I have discussed the philosophy of Lonergan so far in terms of the two limiting assumptions of the Greek-Western philosophical

163

tradition. These two assumptions have traditionally met in the half-way house of the theory of truth. It is, therefore, only logical, as Frederick Crowe has realized, that the key divergence between Lonergan's thought and my own opinions is to be found in the doctrine of truth. But note that there is a lack of symmetry between Lonergan's criticism of my theory of truth and my criticism of his—I wish to call attention to it because it is instructive. The asymmetry is that Lonergan thinks that I am inconsistent and, therefore, incorrect, whereas I think his view is consistent, but nevertheless invalid. What is the significance of this?

Lonergan is consistent when, in the light of the classical principles to which, as I have shown, he adheres, he finds it necessary (and patent through a *reductio ad absurdum*) to understand truth as the adequation of the mind to being, "the correspondence between meaning and meant." [17] But Lonergan thinks that when I assert a different conception of truth there is a contradiction between what I assert and what I in fact do when I *assert* it. That is, he believes he detects a contradiction between the content of my affirmation about the nature of truth (or, for that matter, the content of any affirmation about the nature of truth which contradicted the correspondence theory of truth) and the implication of my act of so affirming. In his own words, Lonergan believes that when I said that truth was something other than the correspondence of meaning and meant, I "overlooked the fact that [I] needed a correspondence view of truth to mean what [I] said." [18] Indeed, he seems to find it amusing that I have "managed to reject [the correspondence view of truth] without apparently adverting to it." [19]

[17] *Ibid.,* p. 74.
[18] *Ibid.,* p. 73.
[19] *Ibid.,* p. 73.

Dogmatism aside, this is instructive, I say, because it helps one pinpoint one of the most important reasons why Lonergan finds it impossible to transcend the two classical metaphysical assumptions to which I have referred and which coalesce in the classical concept of truth. For Lonergan's argument, his *reductio ad absurdum,* his suggestion that the very act of asserting anything implies and conveys the correspondence view of truth, rests upon a certain understanding of the nature of assertion—and, thus, upon a certain understanding of the nature of language. For according to Lonergan the correspondence between the judging mind and being is paralleled by, embodied in, and discernible through, the correspondence between meaning and the meant: "we objectify the self by meaning the self, and we objectify the world by meaning the world. Such meaning of its nature is related to a meant, and what is meant may or may not correspond to what in fact is so. If it corresponds, the meaning is true. If it does not correspond, the meaning is false. Such is the correspondence view of truth." [20] The intentionality of the judging mind is outwardly expressed (presumably not in order to think, but in order to communicate what one has already thought) in the meaning or signification of the assertions made by the speaking mind. This is, of course, the very view which follows from Parmenides, as Plato explicitly concluded, and as Aristotle actually stated in a text we met at the beginning of these lectures: "spoken words are the signs of mental experience and written words are the signs of spoken words. Just as all men have not the same writing, so all men have not the same speech sounds, but the mental experiences, which these directly signify, are the same for all, as also are those things of which our experiences are the images." [21] From which naturally

[20] *Ibid.,* p. 73.
[21] *On Interpretation,* 1 (16 a 3 ff.).

follows in turn that "to say of what is that it is not, or of what is not that it is, is false, while to say of what is that it is, and of what is not that it is not, is true." [22]

The self-evidence of the correspondence concept of truth is actually its self-implication in the view of language as a system of signs. The correspondence concept of truth is thus better described as the semantic concept of truth. And the self-validation of this idea of truth is but the self-consistency of the classical interpretation of the nature of language in the light of the classical epistemological and metaphysical elaborations of the self-concept of the typically Greek religious consciousness. But this view of language, however self-consistent, ancient and honourable, is not above criticism: it is indeed very difficult to maintain in view of linguistic, psychological, anthropological and philosophical research. I have suggested in this book how it may be possible to understand the nature of language in a way other than Aristotle's, not as the expression of thought, but as its creative form, its womb or matrix, as it were, so that language, instead of corresponding to that which is spoken about (as meaning corresponds to the meant) is rather the means whereby consciousness can think meaningfully about a reality that does not have any meaning in or within itself.

Lonergan would find it impossible to admit not only the truth, but even the cogency, of this proposition, since for him "the true statement (concerning objects) intends to state what would be so even if the subject making the statement did not exist." [23] For Lonergan would not simply disagree; he could find no meaning corroborated by a meant in the statement that, unless someone

[22] *Metaphysics*, IV, 7 (1011 b 26).
[23] "The Future of Christianity," p. 5.

were to mean it, there could be no meaning in the meant. This is why he can even find some sport in his interpellation of me: Have I not written a book? Well, then, did I or did I not mean what I wrote? Or would I wish to maintain, perhaps, that I really meant "something else"? Or could it be that I meant "nothing at all"? [24]

In this and in earlier books I have developed an alternative view of language, reality and truth which may or may not be correct but which is probably not altogether inane. I will not repeat it here, or attempt to show how it avoids the difficulties which plague the traditional corresponding views. I will recall, however, that in my interpretation language does not tell what reality is like, and meaning is not the expression of the cognitive relation of the mind to reality, but the formal condition of the possibility of cognitive self-relation to reality. I meant what I wrote. But *this* does not mean that I intended my words to be a depiction of the world. I intended them to facilitate my own understanding of the world, and hopefully my readers'. It is by that standard that I would wish their value to be judged.

I believe I have adequately shown that there is a world of difference between Lonergan's fundamental epistemological position and my own; this is why we also differ in our respective conclusions concerning the future of Christianity and the orientation it should take. How could it be otherwise, if we disagree on the meaning of reality and truth? It is understandable, as I have said, if we in the Hellenic-Western tradition have since time immemorial, for linguistic and other reasons, confused truth and conformity, and believed that inner necessities rule all things. But at the present stage of the evolution of human consciousness it has

[24] *Debate*, p. 73.

become imperative that we proceed to develop our understanding (in all areas, but especially in what pertains to epistemology and metaphysics) from a more critical interpretation of the nature of language than we have assumed in the past. I do not criticize Lonergan on the ground that, having attempted to do this, he has failed. The deficiency of his philosophy is that he has not even attempted it.

But I would not want these remarks on Lonergan's philosophy to end on a simply negative note. My opinion that Lonergan's "main project" provides a doctrine of reality and truth which is no longer sufficiently adequate for our day takes nothing away from my conviction that Lonergan's philosophical creativity is not lightly to be dismissed. For Lonergan is indeed a rarity: he is an original thinker. And in Catholic philosophical circles during the last two centuries or so this is hardly the sort of achievement that marks every midsummer's day. Yet more rare, and a tribute to his character as much as to his thought, is his ability to have inspired (along, to be sure, with uncritical admirers and disciples in the traditional style) a group of scholars composed, without a doubt, of the single most creative, productive, active and hopeful array of talent in philosophy and systematic theology in North American Catholic circles today. For all my criticism, then, of Lonergan's thought, and for all my doubts that his philosophy could provide the bases of more than religious "renewal" during an age when, as I believe, rapid, self-initiated evolution is actually called for—but I have put it badly, it is not called for, it is already happening, and the only question is whether it will continue to come about blindly or aforethought—I would hope that the scarce, valuable resources of North American Catholic thought were not dissipated, and indeed that they were put to efficient, co-operative use.

All intellectual enterprise at all times, but perhaps today more urgently than ever, requires the concourse of many minds. May not the Lonerganians and—what shall I call them?—yes, the "independents," find it possible to collaborate? On one's side, although one hesitates, one need not be forever detained by the remnants of discipleship one sometimes detects even among some of the critical Lonerganians. For one gladly observes, however much one may take issue, for instance, with the very views of language, truth and reality I have criticized here, that among North American Catholic philosophers Lonergan's students stand out as a group in at least one respect: they are alive and well, and living in the twentieth century. It is not of every other Catholic movement that the same could be said.

At the same time, however, one would like earnestly to suggest to Lonerganians that not only the twentieth century but the entire civilization known as Western Christendom is coming to an end— an end which may be all the more conclusive because it is not catastrophic but evolutionary, so that it is at the same time the beginning of a new world. It may not be too early to begin to lay the theoretical foundations of the religious world, I do not say of the twenty-first century, but of at least the twenty-fifth. And one might also remind them that the collaboration of Christian thinkers would not be as aptly sought on the basis of common agreement on any given philosophical or theological doctrine, as, first, on the basis of a common devotion to the religious and human community that their profession serves, and, second, upon their common vision of the tasks which their intellectual service should therefore undertake. But these stipulations probably ask of all but a few exceptional Lonerganians—or so one fears—rather more than they appear ready to concede at this time.

169

Index

Agnostician, 132

Analysis, linguistic, 46–47

Aquinas, St. Thomas, 53–55, 57, 147, 151–152, 156, 158; *see also* Thomism

Arianism, 17

Aristotle, 29–32, 34, 37, 39, 41, 45–47, 49–50, 64, 69, 71, 93, 147, 154, 165–166; *see also* Language, semantic concept of

Augustine of Hippo, St., 154

Authority: crisis of, 108–110; and faith, 104–105; papal, 17; teaching, 26, 108, 111–112; teaching, institution of, 109; teaching, and leadership, 117–118, 125; teaching, limitations of, 120–123; teaching, nature of, 111–125; teaching, and nature of truth, 108, 110, 117, 120–124; teaching, problems of, today, 128–129; teaching, responsibilities of, 118; *see also* Magisterium

Ayer, A. J., 158

Baum, Gregory, 149

Being, contingency of, 53; *see also* Reality, factuality of

Belief: foundations (presuppositions) of, 18–19, 24, 127; *see also* Faith; Reality; Truth

Berkeley, George, 55

Boas, Franz, 40

Burke, T. Patrick, 100

Catholic Church: crisis of, 16–26, 98, 107, 127; history of, 18, 114, 133; nature of, 119–120; teaching of, 25–26; *see also* Authority, teaching; Christianity; Religion

Celibacy, clerical, 17, 26

Certainty: nature of, 52; problem of, 54–57; *see also* Scepticism

Children, rearing of, 118

Chomsky, Noam, 38–39, 69

Christianity: and diversity of forms, 16; evolution of, 147; and human development, 129; unity of, 15–16; *see also* Catholic Church; Religion

Codes, *see* Language

Communication, *see* Language, reduction of, to communication

Conscience, and authority, 109–110

Consciousness: evolution of, 10, 132, 134, 167; properties of, 74; religious, 99, 102; semantic concept of, 41, 51; *see also* Knowledge; Truth; Error; Language

Contraception, morality of, 17, 21, 25–26

Convention, linguistic, *see* Language, conventionality of
Crisis, Catholic, *see* Catholic Church, crisis of
Crowe, Frederick, 159, 164
Crowley, Mrs. Patrick, 21–22

Darwin, Charles, 23
Derrida, Jacques, 41
Descartes, René, 55, 147, 154, 158
Determinism, historical, *see* History, determinism of; Fate
Dogma, conceptualization of, 23
Dogmatism, 62, 163, 165

Ecumenism, 15–16
Error: man's increased capacity for, 116–117; nature of, 59–62, 97–98; possibility of, 59; *see also* Truth; Knowledge; Consciousness
Ethics, political, 117, 143; *see also* War, thermonuclear
Evil, meaning of, 131, 140–142
Evolution and language, 33–37, 39, 73; *see also* Consciousness, evolution of; Religion, evolution of

Faith: and authority, 104–105; ecclesial character of, 103–104; as form of experience, 101–102, 127–128; and knowledge, 99; nature of, 99–104; traditional Catholic doctrine of, 99–100; and truth, 99–100; *see also* Belief; Revelation; Religion
Falsity, *see* Error
Fate, 134–135, 138–140, 143; *see also* Reality, necessity of; History, determinism of

Fitting, Peter, 12
Freedom, *see* Man, freedom of; History, freedom of
Fundamentalism, 109, 111–112

Galileo, 23
Gilson, Étienne, 147
God: belief in, 132; benevolence of, 135–138, 140; development of concept of, 133; nature of, 17, 19, 112, 130–144; providence of, 130–144; self-communication of, 19, 112; will of, 130, 143

Heaven, 139–140, 144
Hegel, Georg Wilhelm Friedrich, 55, 147, 154
Hell, 139–140
Heraclitus, 64
History: determinism of, 137–139; freedom (or contingency) of, 138–141; providential outcome of, 131; *see also* Fate
Hjelmslev, Louis, 40, 69
Humanae Vitae, 25–26
Humboldt, Wilhelm von, 39
Hume, David, 55

John (the Evangelist), 142
John XXIII, Pope, 117

Kant, Immanuel, 55, 147
Knowledge: and faith, 99; fallibility of human, 54–55; nature of, 51, 82, 85, 121–122, 159; traditional (or semantic) concept of, 56–58, 94, 147, 149–152, 161; *see also* Truth; Error; Consciousness

Language: reduction of, to communication, 32, 44–45, 66–69; and codes, 43; and consciousness, 79; conventionality of, 30–36, 40; cultural relativity of, 40–41, 70–71; effect of literacy on, 46–50; effect of communications technology on, 48–49; and evolution, 33–37, 39, 73; and evolution of religion, 10; as expression, 40, 49, 70, 72, 95–96; as form of thought, 40–41, 44, 69–70, 96; and grammatical rules, 42; and human nature, 32–33; as innate faculty, 37–39; learning, 30–33, 37–42, 70–71; and music, 75–77; nature of, 166–168; and objectivity, 86; relation of, to reality, 44, 78, 86, 96–97; relation of, to thought, 12, 30–31, 41, 49, 64–74; as self- communication, 86; as self-relation to reality, 75, 77, 90, 95–96; and signification, 43; and society, 32; as syntactic system, 78; traditional (or semantic, or Aristotelian) concept of, 29–62, 64–65, 69–71, 74–75, 78, 80, 86, 93–95, 164, 166; translation of, 63–64; and vocabulary, 42–43; and writing, 30, 47–49, 63–64

Leibniz, Gottfried Wilhelm von, 154

Locke, John, 55

Lonergan, Bernard J. F., 12, 146–169

Magisterium: abuse of, 128; nature of, 25–26, 111–125; responsibilities of, 124–125; submission to, 108–110; see also Authority, teaching

Man: changes in nature of, 129; nature of, 32–33, 89–90; freedom of, 131, 136–137, 141

Maritain, Jacques, 147–148, 150

Marriage, ends of, 25

McLuhan, H. Marshall, 45–46, 48, 63

Morality, nature of, 141–143

Papacy, adequate characteristics of, today, 125

Parmenides, 160–161, 165

Paul VI, Pope, 107–109, 117, 125

Pelagianism, 137

Philosophy: Catholic, 145, 168–169; Greek, 52–53, 55–56, 134–136, 147–148; historical nature of, 156–158; history of, 155, 158; and revelation, 19–21, 23–24

Plato, 31, 147, 154, 165

Predestination, 136–137

Providence, see God, providence of; Fate

Reality: Christian attitude towards, 53; factuality (or contingency) of, 81–88; necessity of, 52–53, 87, 134–136; and process, 89; traditional (or semantic) concept of, 41, 93–94, 147; and truth, 97–98

Reformation, Protestant, 17, 103–104

Relativism, cultural, 41

Religion: and evolution, 10, 16, 128, 138, 141, 143–144; evolution of, 10, 147, 168; Greek, 52, 87; natural, 111; nature of, 10, 101–102; revealed, 19–21, 111; and sexuality, 25–26; see also Catholic Church; Christianity; Faith; Revelation

Renewal, inadequacy of Catholic, 146, 168

Revelation: fundamentalist concept of, 111; nature of, 19, 112–113; and philosophy, 19–21, 23–24; *see also* Faith; Religion

Rosenstock-Huessy, Eugen, 41

Russell, Bertrand, 47, 93

Ryle, Gilbert, 158

Sapir, Edward, 40

Saussure, Ferdinand de, 39–40, 69

Scepticism, 62; *see also* Certainty

Schillebeeckx, Edward, 100

Schism, East-West, 17

Sexuality, and religion, 25–26

Sign, linguistic, 30–31, 36, 38, 44, 50, 72; *see also* Language; Signification; Symbol

Signification, linguistic, 45, 49, 57, 60, 69, 86; *see also* Language; Sign

Sin: actual, 139; original, 17

Socrates, 115

Speech, *see* Language

Stoicism, 134–136

Strawson, Peter F., 46

Structuralism, 38

Symbol, and sign, 30

Syntax, relation of, to semantics, 42

Teaching: nature of, 115–116; traditional concept of, 110–111

Thales, 87, 162

Thomas Aquinas, St., *see* Aquinas, St. Thomas; Thomism

Thomism: traditional, 146; transcendental, 146–169

Thought: nature of, 50; relation of language to, 12, 30–31, 41, 49, 64–74; relation of writing to, 49; voicing of, 65, 67, 69, 73; *see also* Language; Consciousness

Translation, *see* Language, translation of

Truth: and certainty, 54; and doctrinal change, 19–26, 127, 129; and factuality, 81–85; and language, 12, 51–62, 78, 80–81; nature of, 25, 51, 79–82, 84–85, 87, 96–98, 115–116, 121–122, 164; pursuit of, 116; as quality of consciousness, 97; and reality, 97–98; and revelation, 19–22; traditional (or semantic) concept of, 24, 51–62, 78, 80–81, 95–96, 98, 121–122, 162–166; *see also* Error, Knowledge; Consciousness; Language

Unity, Christian, 15–16

War, thermonuclear, 129–131, 143–144

Whorf, Benjamin, 40

Wittgenstein, Ludwig, 46

World, end of, 17, 129–131

Writing, *see* Language

Date Due

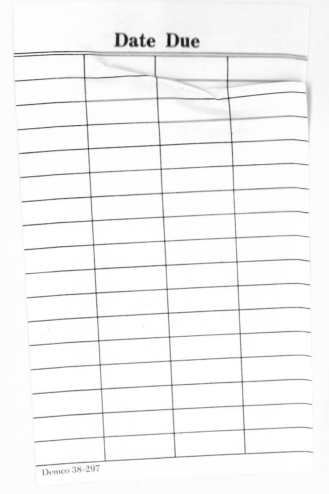